D1405038

MUIR WOODS
NATIONAL MONUMENT

by John Hart

Introduction by Edgar Wayburn

GOLDEN GATE NATIONAL PARKS CONSERVANCY
SAN FRANCISCO, CALIFORNIA

Introduction copyright © 2011 by Golden Gate National Parks Conservancy
Text copyright © 2011 by John Hart

All rights reserved. No part of this book may be reproduced or transmitted
in any form or by any means without written permission from the publisher.
Address all queries to Golden Gate National Parks Conservancy, Bldg 201
Fort Mason, 3rd Floor, San Francisco, California 94123.
www.parksconservancy.org

ISBN 978-1-9325-1909-9

Library of Congress Control Number: 2010931315

Project and Art Direction: Robert Lieber
Design and Photography Acquisition: Vivian Young
National Park Service Advisor: Mia Monroe
Editor: Susan Tasaki
Production: Sarah Lau
Cartography: Stephen Skartvedt

Printed in Hong Kong on FSC Certified paper using soy-based inks

*In long plain lines the redwoods rise,
toward wind noise, or toward silence.*

John Hart

Contents

Introduction

I am just slightly older than Muir Woods National Monument. When President Theodore Roosevelt proclaimed the monument, on January 9, 1908, I was a little over one year old, an infant in faraway Georgia.

In the summer of 1933 I settled in San Francisco and quickly connected to the wild country north of the city. I particularly enjoyed taking the ferry across the water to the southern end of Marin County, then the train to Mill Valley, Corte Madera, or Larkspur—in those days, small villages nestled at the foot of Mount Tamalpais, whose green slopes offered the greatest possible refuge to an urban dweller. It was then that I first saw the great trees along Redwood Creek that William Kent and Theodore Roosevelt had saved. I was grateful to those leaders for a job well done. Or was it done?

Returning after military service in World War II, I saw suburbs fanning out across the land. Even rugged Mount Tamalpais was not immune. Muir Woods National Monument, a small Mount Tamalpais State Park, and the Marin Municipal Water District lands protected parts of it, but I learned that much of the land I took such pleasure walking over was private and open to development—which in fact was beginning.

One Sunday afternoon in 1947, while hiking above Muir Woods, I sat down in the grass and thought about what an ideal park on this flank of the mountain might contain. The entire watershed of Redwood Creek—that is, the land and waters from ridge to ridge—should be protected.

I didn't realize how closely I was walking in the footsteps of William Kent, who donated Muir Woods to the nation and dreamed of something even grander, a Mount Tamalpais National Park. I also didn't realize that I was embarking on a sixty-year conservation career that would take me to the mightier groves of Redwood National Park in far northern California, to the wildlands of Alaska, and also back again and again to Tamalpais and what I call "the hills of home."

Along the way my watershed vision grew. By 1960 I was dreaming of an unbroken stretch of public lands leading out of San Francisco and north through Marin over Mount Tamalpais to Point Reyes National Seashore. In 1972, with the creation of the Golden Gate National Recreation Area, that goal was achieved. Muir Woods is now just one corner—albeit a very special corner—in a vast complex of parks, both north and south of the Golden Gate, totaling some 180,000 acres.

But it would be fair to say that Muir Woods is where it all began.

Ed Wayburn

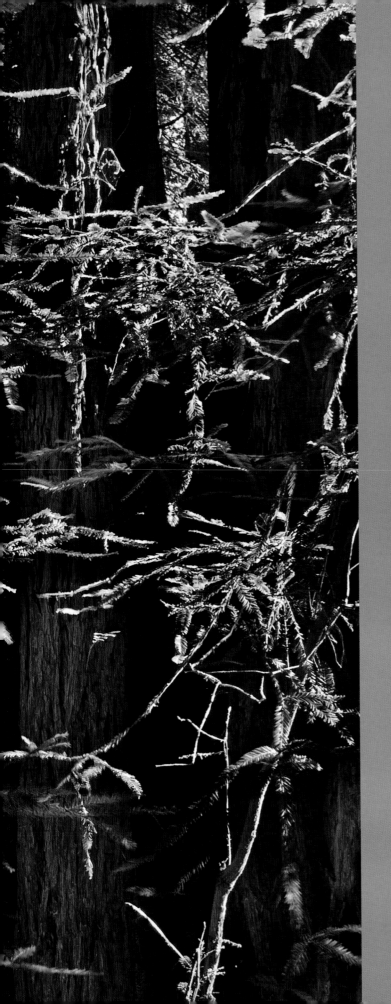

One
REDWOOD FOREST

In long plain lines the redwoods rise, toward wind noise, or toward silence. They rise clear out of the place you walk in, the one made green and ferny by their shade. With their enormous height—few of the tops can really be seen—the massive red-brown boles seem almost spindly. Around their bases the visitors flock, and angle their necks to see, and click their cameras, and ask and answer.

Die Muir-Wälder. Muir Woods National Monument. *Le Monument National de Muir Woods*: brochures tell the story in four alphabets, eight languages; there is demand for as many more. Listen a few minutes at the entrance on a Saturday, and you'll hear a good number of these tongues.

One of the first parks ever set aside for the coast redwood, named for a

great and talkative conservationist who had little to do with its saving, Muir Woods now is an emblem. It represents the redwoods in a way in which other and greater redwood parks, on other and greater redwood-bordered streams farther away from the city, do not. For multitudes over the decades, these redwoods, so close to San Francisco and a stop on numerous tours, have been *the* redwoods: perhaps the only ones they will ever see.

Yet it is possible to walk through Muir Woods quickly and take in rather little, to come away with nothing but a vague sense of coolness and postcard grandeur. That's inevitable, even appropriate. This is a place where nothing happens fast. In a forest of *Sequoia sempervirens*, time itself is the amazement; slowness, the very marvel.

Redwood Time: The Well of the Past

Just into Muir Woods a mounted exhibit tells time, redwood-fashion. It is a cross-section of a tree just over a thousand years old. Until 1988, a cheerfully Anglocentric display picked out annual growth rings corresponding to the Battle of Hastings, the Magna Carta. Now we have Western Hemisphere events, from the founding of the Native American city at Mesa Verde to Columbus and beyond, encompassed in the lifetime of one tree.

We're meant to marvel at that thousand years, and do. But neither the Magna Carta nor Mesa Verde is anything but the very latest news—on the redwood scale of years.

Unlike the higher animals, unlike many other plants, redwoods apparently have no fixed lifespan. As they get older, their growth slows down, they produce fewer viable seeds, but their basic functions continue unimpaired. "Immortal" is too strong a word, yet this huge fact remains: there is no built-in reason why any particular redwood tree need ever die.

> *...very few other trees are as good as a redwood at defending themselves against natural enemies that limit potential lives.*

A look through the plant world shows that this open-ended life is not unique. The Douglas-fir trees that grow here and there in Muir Woods National Monument, for instance, could theoretically last millennia. But very few other trees are as good as a redwood at defending themselves against natural enemies that limit potential lives. A Douglas-fir loses a branch in a high wind; a fungus invades at the break; the end begins. A redwood with a broken limb or even a snapped-off crown is no more mortally ill than a human with a broken arm.

There are some redwood-eaters—a few species of fungus that colonize parts of the tree, a few beetles and borers that can pierce to the sapwood. But none of these do serious damage to a mature tree. Something about the wood—perhaps the particular form of tannin it contains, though the matter is poorly understood—resists invaders. Ecologist Stephen Veirs writes simply: "No killing diseases are known for established trees."

No killing diseases. Those short-lived, two-legged, rather noisy creatures down there among the ferns and elk clover—large-brained enough to look up and wonder, smart enough, too, to know what a lifespan is—can think about that for a moment, if they choose.

Of course, accidents, chiefly involving wind and fire (not to mention logging), do occur. They happen frequently enough to limit the lifespan of the trees, in a practical sense. Time runs out for a redwood, too. But it is not Time itself that does the harm.

Seeds, Burls, and Sprouts

Going by ring-counts, even the coast redwood is not the longest-lived plant species known. Its cousin the giant sequoia, *Sequoiadendron giganteum*, a native of the Sierra Nevada range, reaches 3,000 years; the bristlecone pine of the White Mountains and other mountaintops out in the arid expanses between the Sierra Nevada and the Rocky Mountains approaches 5,000. But tree rings do not tell the whole story.

Redwoods have two ways of reproducing. Some new trees begin with the seeds that drop, in fall and early winter, from insignificant-appearing cones. Redwoods, however, don't put much energy into sexual reproduction. Seeds are small and most of them in fact are sterile. For this species, seeding is a secondary means of securing the future. The forest perpetuates itself primarily through another mechanism, sprouting.

Almost from the moment it breaks out of the seed, a redwood seedling begins building what is called a burl ring. This is a dense mass of living shoots whose growth is begun but, for the moment, suppressed. As the tree establishes itself, the burl ring sinks into the soil. As the trunk expands, the ring widens with it and forms a heavy sheath both above and below the ground. But the upward growth of the incipient sprouts continues to be curbed by a regulatory chemical.

If the parent tree gets into trouble, the natural brake is released. Sprouts from the burl ring explode toward the light. All at once, around the base of the stricken trunk, a ring of new shoots appears.

These burl-ring sprouts have a great advantage over plants beginning from seed: even when millimeters thick themselves, they have the root system of a mighty tree to feed them. They can wait decades, if necessary, to struggle up into the forest canopy, and they do.

And so arises the characteristic phenomenon of the sprout ring: circles of great trees surrounding an older tree, or a stump, or a vacancy. These rings are sometimes called "family circles." But the trees of the circle are not separate individuals, genetically related: they are parts of a single individual, connected at the root, thrust up from the burl ring of a single ancient stem whose root is still alive. The actual plant is this community of stems, this interconnected clone.

Redwood clones occur in other patterns than simple rings. A successful stem in one circle often in due course becomes the center of a new, younger circle, producing a pattern of overlapping arcs of trees. Less commonly, successor trees occur in lines. Fallen redwoods have the ability to sprout anywhere along their length, and clones have been found as far as 40 meters outside the obvious clusters.

How old is a redwood clone? Is it only as old as the annual rings in its bole? Or is it as old as the older tree it derives from? And if age is measured by the root, just how old might such a redwood be?

There are precedents. Creosote bushes, growing in redwood-like rings in the Mojave Desert, are thought to have common roots six or seven thousand years old. Some groups of aspens—which likewise are multi-stemmed trees, not stands of separate individuals—may be 8,000 years old at the root. Living coast redwood roots may reach ages as great as either creosote bushes or aspens—or greater. Somewhere in California, unidentified, there may grow a redwood that is the oldest living woody plant in the world.

> ...the trees of the circle are not separate
> individuals, genetically related: they are parts of
> a single individual, connected at the root, thrust
> up from the burl ring of a single ancient stem
> whose root is still alive.

Why Bother with Seeds?

This greatest of conifers has one of the smallest of cones, less than an inch wide and long. This is not an incidental fact but rather, reflects the low priority redwoods put on sexual reproduction. Like other conifers, redwoods rely on wind to get pollen from stamen to flower, but pollen output is skimpier than in other species, and many ovules are never fertilized. The autumn seed drop is variable from year to year and from tree to tree, amounting at best to about a hundred small, brown, flattened seeds per cone. Fewer than 10 percent germinate, and only a very few seedlings survive the attack of fungus in the moist litter of the forest floor. Trace back the history of a given redwood trunk and you are much more likely to find a sprout than a seed. What, then, do the trees need this form of reproduction for?

The answer is: insurance, of two kinds. The new plants that result from the union of a pollen grain and an ovule will differ genetically from each other, as sprouts will not. Faced with a new disease or other special challenge, some offspring inevitably survive better than others, providing more chances for the species to survive. We can see this happening today among oak trees afflicted with Sudden Oak Death.

Seeds also are better than sprouts at colonizing fresh ground. Wherever mineral soil is exposed—for instance, where a tree has fallen, or where a flood has either removed organic litter or buried it with silt—seedlings appear and thrive. They also sprout on downed logs where debris and dust have settled to form pockets of soil. And if some global catastrophe were to wipe out the standing trees and existing roots, seeds would provide an alternate route to survival. Such rebirths from seed may have happened more than once in the extraordinary career of *Sequoia sempervirens*.

Sequoia sempervirens

Sequoiadendron giganteum

Lumping and Splitting

The coast redwood used to be a member of the baldcypress family of trees, the Taxodiaceae. Now it is just a cypress, a member of a much more extensive group called the Cupressaceae. The species, of course, has not changed, but our understanding of its family relationships has.

Such reshufflings have been going on ever since the Swede Carl Linnaeus developed his hierarchical system for classifying life forms, the scheme that, much refined, is still in use today. Its ultimate units are the species, which have two-part names: a genus label that may be shared among several close relatives, and a species label that pins identity down. Thus, *Sequoia sempervirens*, *Sequoiadendron giganteum*. The next wider grouping above the genus is the subfamily: for the redwoods this is Sequoioideae. Then comes the family: Cupressaceae. Above the family are at least nine other levels, culminating in vast "kingdoms" and still vaster "domains" of living things.

The whole Linnean structure is designed to reflect the way organisms evolved. All the cypresses presumably go back to a common ancestor, but the details are subject to revision. Groups are constantly being merged or divided, processes science calls "lumping" and "splitting." Coast redwood and the giant sequoia were once in the same *Sequoia* genus, but have been split. Cypresses and baldcypresses were once in two families, but have been lumped. The process continues up and down the levels of the classification scheme. In recent years, precise analysis of DNA has helped clarify degrees of relationship and resolved many of these debates, seemingly for good.

Drifting Through Time

But the well of the past suggested by that round slab of cut redwood is far deeper than the life of any individual tree, however you count it.

Perhaps because it reproduces so much by sprout, without the reshuffling of genes that goes with sexual reproduction, the redwood stands out among plants as an inveterate and—in its current, restricted range—triumphant conservative. In a changing world, as mountains rise and fall, as continents shift and jostle, the redwoods have changed rather little.

Redwoods belong to the ancient plant family of the cypresses, the Cupressaceae. Cypress relatives include the cedars, cypresses, and junipers, and are found all over the world, but the group contains only 130 or so individual species. As a lineage the cypresses are rather thin-spread, like a proud old clan producing few children. The subfamily Sequoioideae contains the three species known as redwoods: the coast redwood, *Sequoia sempervirens*; the giant sequoia of the Sierra Nevada, *Sequoiadendron giganteum*; and the dawn redwood of China, *Metasequoia glyptostroboides*.

Those mouthfuls of names need parsing. The coast redwood got its scientific name in 1847 from the Austrian botanist Stephen Endlicher. The second word, the species name, means "evergreen." In coining the first word, the genus name, Endlicher passed up the chance to honor himself, as botanists are prone to do. Instead, he apparently chose to commemorate a celebrated Native American, the Cherokee scholar Sequoyah (1770s–1843), at right. Sequoyah was known throughout the Western world for devising a unique set of symbols for the writing of his native language. Though Sequoyah never saw a redwood tree, the naming has a certain rightness. His syllabary gave his people a powerful tool in their fight for cultural survival, and redwoods are a symbol of what lasts.

The other two redwood species are derivatively named. *Sequoiadendron giganteum* is simply the gigantic sequoia tree, and the dawn redwood's name can be translated as the sequoia-like tree with carved cones, a reference to the distinctive grooved surface of the unripened fruit.

Present range of Coast Redwood

Present range of Giant Sequoia

Present range of Dawn Redwood

FOSSIL RECORD ·····

- Coast Redwood
  Sequoia sempervirens

▲ Giant Sequoia
  Sequoiadendron giganteum

▼ Dawn Redwood
  Metasequoia glyptostroboides

Redwoods not very different from those in California appear in the fossil record some 144 million years ago, in the period called the Cretaceous—dinosaur days. Most sequoia fossils are found across the Northern Hemisphere at middle latitudes, in Japan and Kazakhstan and France and all across the United States. During the first half of the redwoods' career, all of these places were parts of a single vast northern continent, Laurasia. Laurasia, it seems, was redwood country, and the southern parts of it were the domain of a tree a visitor to Muir Woods would instantly recognize.

Since the first Sequoia forests lifted their domes and spires to the sky, mountains great and small, thousands of them, have been weathered, ground away and cast into the sea.

The slow brute dance of the continents and oceanic plates has since shaped us a world cooler, drier, and more rugged than the one in which the redwoods reached their prime. Beginning about 25 million years ago, western North America began to buckle and rift, forming lofty plateaus, deserts, and mountain chains: barriers of chill and aridity between the Pacific and the Atlantic worlds. The redwoods to the east failed to survive. The redwoods to the west shifted their range repeatedly in response to changing climate. Today they occupy only this coastal strip, never more than forty-five miles deep and about five hundred miles long, on the far western edge of the westernmost fragment of old Laurasia. In the Eastern Hemisphere, only the relict population of dawn redwoods in China now represents the redwood tribe.

It's always a stretch to imagine geologic time, to conceive of the planet's solid surfaces as bustling and fluid. It jolts the awareness again to encounter living forms that have outlasted not only their live contemporaries but even the basic continental shapes they evolved with. The redwoods are not the only such—the horsetails along the creek in Muir Woods go back further even than do the trees above—but it would be hard to imagine survivors more dramatic than these high red forms. John Muir, responding in 1908 to the news that the grove was to be named for him, went straight to the point:

> *A Sierra peak also and one of the Alaska glaciers bear my name, but these aboriginal woods, barring human action, will outlast them all. Since the first Sequoia forests lifted their domes and spires to the sky, mountains great and small, thousands of them, have been weathered, ground away and cast into the sea; while two of the many species of Sequoia have come safely though all the geological changes and storms that have fallen upon them since Cretaceous times.*

Sequoia Superlatives

As well as being among the oldest living things, *Sequoia sempervirens* provides the tallest, the thickest, and some of the most massive specimens of living matter on earth.

The tallest trees yet found, approaching 380 feet, stand far north of Muir Woods, in Redwood National Park near the Oregon border. The thickest tree known today is a Sierran giant sequoia, but stumps show that some cut-down coast redwoods had even greater "diameters at breast height," the standard measure. When total wood volume is measured, certain of the coast redwoods, called "titans," are at or near the top of the planetary list. And redwood forests at their climax are literally the heaviest in the world: not even tropical forests generate this mass of living matter per acre or hectare.

The upper region of a very large redwood tree is its own small world. When wind breaks off the leading tip of a tree, it sends out new trunks from below the break to rise alongside the old axis, a process called "reiteration." Where these new stems rub against each other, they often fuse together again, producing a kind of irregular cage. Debris readily catches at junctions and breaks down into pockets of soil. Mosses, fungi, and even sapling trees of several species can establish themselves in these pockets.

How can redwoods get so tall? Any tree must pump water up from the ground, a process driven by what is called capillary action—the tendency of a liquid to climb upward in a narrow tube—and by the slight vacuum created as moisture evaporates from leaves. But there are limits to this water transport, and the tallest redwoods seem to transgress them all. Scientists now think they know how it's done. It has to do with the subtle force of nature that almost defines *Sequoia sempervirens* country: fog.

Trees of Fog

There is fog over Muir Woods this morning: moving in the tops of the trees, dampening hillside meadows, milling among the boles. A visitor asks: "Are you going to get any sun in here today?" Maybe. Maybe not. But if you find the fog dreary, you are not a redwood tree.

Mist droplets catch and coalesce on needles and leaves, sifting down in what is called "fog-drip."

Redwoods require an equable climate and cannot endure cold, heat, or very much wind. Most of all, they must have a lot of water, all the time. Only at the far northern end of the species' range is rainfall sufficient and distributed well enough throughout the year to give them what they need. If there were no other source of moisture, by August the soil would be dry enough to start killing the redwoods in most groves, certainly those at Muir Woods.

But not long after the rains taper off, the summer fogs begin to push in off the nearby sea. The gray masses move in in the afternoon and burn off in the morning, on some days barely admitting the pale outline of the sun. The hotter it is inland, the more likely the coast is to be fogged in; clear days are also relatively cool.

By keeping temperatures low, the fog slows evaporation from needles and ground. It also, and much more importantly, brings in a large new water supply. Mist droplets catch and coalesce on needles and leaves, sifting down in what is called "fog-drip." This is thought to contribute, at the very least, the equivalent of ten inches of summer rain. All trees benefit, but some trees are better at catching fog than others. The structure of a redwood crown, with its many branches and fine-textured needles, is ideal. So is its great size. The fog comb is both efficient and very large.

And, in a final twist, redwoods apparently use the fog to sustain the
height that helps them harvest it. Scientists have concluded that the lofty tips
are nourished in part by water absorbed from the air around them, saving the
energy cost of pulling it up from the ground. In one mechanism, the parent
tree sends rootlets into the pockets of soil that form aloft to get at the water
there. More importantly, redwoods absorb fog's moisture directly into their
needles, reversing the normal "evapotranspiration" process by which plants
lose water to air. It appears that certain fungi, symbiotically resident in the
needles, help the process along.

Just as the enormous upper mass of a redwood tree can be related to
its need for summer water, so can its startlingly puny roots. Redwoods lack
a central taproot. Instead, a mat of smaller roots spreads just below the soil
surface, extending perhaps eighty feet from the trunk. This structure is a
sponge to catch the moisture that drips from the fog-saturated canopy above.

Such a root platform is not terribly stable. In a natural forest, mutual
wind-shelter and interlocking roots keep the trees firm; but if part of the
stand is cut away, trees at the new edge will topple by the dozen.

As a rule, large trees suck water from the soil they are rooted in, drying
out the area beneath them. Often, logging will actually increase the flow in
a nearby creek or spring. But redwoods break this rule as they do so many
others. They themselves apparently consume only about a third of the
moisture they wring from the sky. The other two-thirds nourishes other
plants, replenishes groundwater, and runs off into local streams. Redwoods
make their world wetter; cutting them dries it out again.

False turkey tail

Honey mushroom

Oyster mushroom

Golden waxy cap

29

Trees of Fire

These trees of the cool, gray mist not only tolerate but also apparently profit from a completely opposite phenomenon of nature: forest fire.

Redwood bark is very thick—six to twelve inches on a mature tree—and full of moisture. It resists flames well and insulates the cambium, the living layer beneath, from heat. Fire can best get a grip on a redwood where debris has piled against it, usually on its uphill side, providing hours' worth of fuel. Once persistent heat has killed a segment of cambium, later fires can then burn away bark and wood to create a scar, a cavity, or even a hollow big enough to camp in—the pioneers called these "goose-pens." Most often, though, the trunk remains alive.

The occasional singeing prepares the ground for seedlings by burning off some of the forest litter or duff, making it easier for incipient roots to reach the mineral soil beneath, which the flames also enrich with ash.

Over their history, the California redwoods have experienced fire in several different rhythms. Before the arrival of the Asian pioneers we now think of as Native Americans, 8,000 to 10,000 years ago, fire may have been comparatively infrequent. The first human inhabitants probably speeded up the pace, using fire skillfully to encourage the growth of edible or otherwise useful plants and as an occasional aid in hunting.

When the Spanish came to California, one of their first decrees was to outlaw the setting of fires. Two centuries, more or less, of rigorous fire suppression followed. Fire was simply the enemy, at all times to be prevented and extinguished. Then, as these matters began to be studied further in forests around the world, ecologists did a series of double takes.

They came to realize that, in many landscapes, fire is simply inevitable, and that, moreover, the attempt to prevent all fire sometimes only guarantees that more dead wood will be available for an eventual holocaust. They found further that certain forests actually depend on fire for their maintenance. The giant sequoia of the Sierra Nevada, for example, would lose out to other trees if frequent, light fires did not sweep through the groves.

For the coast redwoods, the benefits of fire are less obvious, but they are real. Most notably, fire promotes reproduction by seed, the secondary but still important means by which the redwoods propagate. The occasional singeing prepares the ground for seedlings by burning off some of the forest litter or duff, making it easier for incipient roots to reach the mineral soil beneath, which the flames also enrich with ash. Fire also controls certain disease-causing organisms, like the heartwood rot *Poria sequoiae* and Sudden Oak Death (which lightly afflicts redwoods). Where large redwoods or other trees are actually killed, the resulting openings let sunlight into the forest floor and help seedlings to thrive.

In the long run, fire helps the redwoods simply by hurting them much less than it hurts their competitors. Scientists note that the redwood does not occur north of the line where summers are so cool and wet as to make forest fires a rarity.

Trees of Shade

Even in "redwood country," not every seemingly suitable spot grows a redwood tree. Especially in the southern part of the tree's range, distribution becomes spotty. In addition to adequate rainfall, fog, and moderate temperatures, the trees need several more advantages to thrive. They need wind shelter, both because of the drying effects of wind and because their shallow roots make them easy to topple. They need soils that hold water well; these are typically derived from sandstone. And as an additional safeguard against dryness, redwood trees need shade.

What can put the world's tallest trees in the shade? Only one thing: the land itself.

Look at your shadow in sunlight. If you're standing anywhere north of the tropics, it will always be falling somewhat north of you—northwest in the morning, northeast in the evening, stubbily due north at noon. To put it another way, your north slope is shadier. So it is with hills. Their north-facing sides are shadier, therefore cooler, therefore more humid. And their

northeast sides are even cooler than their northwest
ones, because whatever sun they get is morning
sun, received before the air has gotten warm. In the
high mountains, north and northeast exposures
have lingering snowfields. On the ocean side of the
California Coast Range, you find redwood trees
instead.

*When you're walking in the
shadows of Muir Woods, it seems
that the redwood forest might go
on forever.*

   The upper valley of Redwood Creek on Mount Tamalpais—the place
we know as Muir Woods—illustrates this factor neatly. When you're walking
in the shadows of Muir Woods, it seems that the redwood forest might go on
forever. Leave the canyon floor, however, and you'll quickly see the workings
of sun-angle or "aspect." If you take a trail to the right, you'll be climbing a
south-facing hillside; the redwoods soon give way to a drier mixed-evergreen
forest, with such trees as oaks and orange-barked madrones. On the shadier
slope to your left, the redwoods continue for half a mile, abruptly ceasing only
when a windy ridgeline is neared.

Trees of Flood

Yet another natural force shapes the lives of many redwoods: winter flooding of the streams along which they grow.

The constant restless cycle of an unconfined stream, moving, depositing, and renewing sediments, creates the deep, fertile soil where redwoods flourish. Most (though not all) of the biggest trees grow on alluvial flats along Northern California's Eel River. You can see the same principle in action at Muir Woods. Curving back and forth from hillside to ferny hillside, Redwood Creek defines where the most impressive redwoods are: the giants grow on the fertile alluvial points inside those curves.

In redwood terms, this forest is a youngster. The average lifespan of a big redwood, a redwood that makes it up into the full sunlight of the forest top or "canopy," is apparently about one thousand years.

Streambank flats are a changeable environment. Erosion can tear land away, or deposit drifts of new soil. Redwood roots are adapted to this latter case. When silt deposits raise the ground level, the trunk quickly develops an upper story of rootlets just below the soil surface.

Muir Woods shows us what a redwood forest needs and what a redwood forest is. Annual rainfall here averages about 40 inches, nearly all of it falling between mid-November and mid-April. (Snow is a rarity.) During the summer months, fog becomes the water source for the trees. The winding creek below creates the soil that supports the largest specimens. A ridge blocks the prevailing wind. Now and then there is a rejuvenating flood or fire.

For all their grandeur, the individual trees at the monument do not come near the potential of the species in height, diameter, mass, or crown complexity. The tallest, in the cluster known as Bohemian Grove, reaches a mere 260 feet. The thickest local tree, a little over 13 feet through at chest height, is nearby. So rangers say, but caution that a really thorough inventory has never been done. To prevent trampling at their roots, the record trees are no longer singled out by signs.

In redwood terms, this forest is a youngster. The average lifespan of a big redwood, a redwood that makes it up into the full sunlight of the forest top or "canopy," is apparently about one thousand years. Some trees last twice that long. But in Muir Woods, there are rather few ancient trees and a preponderance of young ones, six hundred years old or less. It's rather like a

human population with almost everybody under forty. Why? There seem to be two possible answers.

First explanation: these redwoods are on the young side because, in this place, they die early. The Redwood Creek valley is less than optimum as redwood habitat. It may simply be a bit too dry here, a bit too windy, a bit too thin of soil, a bit too subject to droughts to allow the trees to reach a typical redwood life.

Second and more dramatic explanation: Muir Woods is young because it is new. The forest, this speculation goes, was largely wiped out sometime in the past millennium; it has been recovering ever since. The disaster might have been a mudslide off the unstable flank of Mount Tamalpais, or it might have been a forest fire of unusual, "stand-clearing" intensity. It would follow perhaps that this is an adolescent redwood forest, with a more magnificent adulthood still ahead of it.

Improving on Nature?

In the hundred years since the decision was made to preserve Muir Woods forever, we have learned a lot about the natural workings of the forest. Modern managers look back with head-shaking sympathy at some of the decisions taken in the earliest years, especially with regard to flooding and fire.

Winter floods provide one of the pulses in the syncopated rhythm of life at Muir Woods. The occasional really big flood event, admittedly, can be alarming. Banks crumble. Streamside alders topple. Even a redwood may be threatened. Today's park rangers regard such dramas as part of the territory, but their predecessors did not. After a memorable deluge in 1924, a campaign was begun to keep the creek in bounds, first of all by keeping it free of fallen branches and debris. "I got everything out but three large stumps before my funds gave out," an early manager wrote proudly.

The taming of Redwood Creek got serious in the 1930s, when the New Deal public works programs brought an army of government-paid labor. Between 1933 and 1938, the Civilian Conservation Corps (CCC) lined almost the entire length of the creek within Muir Woods with rockwork "revetments," handsome mortarless rock banks, still obvious in many places. CCC workers also installed log check dams to replace untidy natural ones, and here and there they dumped a load of boulders to create a scenic artificial rapid. Any debris that got into the stream on its own was zealously removed.

Thirty years later, government researchers in the Pacific Northwest
and elsewhere began to take a serious look at wild creeks and the processes
at work within them. They zeroed in especially on the role of fallen logs and
branches in such streams and found, to put it simply, that untidy streams
work better. They have more water in them in the summer; they handle peak
flows better in the winter; they suffer less erosion; and they contain markedly
more fish. Logs in streams are now considered an essential component of a
healthy forest.

In the 1980s, the new doctrine reached Muir Woods. Since then, the
tendency has been to leave Redwood
Creek to itself, so far as safety permits.
Trees and boughs that fall into the creek
now stay there. When the old rockwork
sheds stones into the stream, there the

*Winter floods provide one of the
pulses in the syncopated rhythm of
life at Muir Woods.*

stones lie. When the creek swirls out of its banks, leaving drifts of silt among
the ferns, the park staff applauds. And if some few visitors wonder why things
aren't kept rather neater (sometimes expressing sympathy: "I guess they cut
your budget, huh?"), they see the point immediately when informed.

Fire, too, has had its up and downs. You don't have to walk far in Muir
Woods to see the marks of past blazes: some trees blackened, some trees
scarred, a few deeply fire hollowed, and several apparently fire killed—but
with sprout circles rising around them. The Coast Miwok inhabitants of

41

the region including Muir Woods undoubtedly burned this area frequently, perhaps as often as once a decade, doing the forest no harm. Then came the era of fire as enemy. The last major blaze appears to have occurred in 1845. One result of successful fire suppression is that the redwood forest has expanded up the hillside to the north. There is no longer a view of the ocean from the Ocean View Trail. Another result is the buildup of leaf litter, brush, and many small trees, alive and dead, in the formerly rather open forest. With all this kindling at the ready, a wildfire now could be much too big for comfort.

The best hope for heading off a major blaze lies in setting a series of minor ones, in cool weather, to consume duff and small-diameter fuels. In 1985, for the first time in 200 years, such controlled fires were ignited in Muir Woods and surrounding public lands. Rangers happily noticed the appearance of many new redwood seedlings in the areas that were singed. In the late 1990s, about a tenth of the monument area, mostly on Deer Park Ridge to the south, was subjected to managed burns. Managers hope soon to bring the flames nearer to the core of the woods.

Controlled burn, 1986

Western azalea

Redwood sorrel

Living with the Redwoods

Redwoods, like all living things, are members of communities formed of thousands of species. Wherever the big trees grow, however, they dominate, in large measure creating the living space for their biotic partners.

Over their long history, these big trees have been the changeless element in ever-changing assemblages of plants and animals. When they first appeared, flowering plants, including broad-leafed trees, had not yet evolved to share their world. On the floor of an early Cretaceous redwood forest you'd have found familiar fungi, mosses, and ferns, less familiar tree ferns and giant horsetails (crushed here and there by the tread of a dinosaur), but no ground-hugging redwood sorrel, no streamside maple trees.

The associates of redwood, so different over time, also differ from place to place within their current range. Muir Woods is the southernmost example of what is called the central redwood forest type, extending from Humboldt County down to the Golden Gate. Here the redwoods mix variously with Douglas-fir, tanoak, California laurel (also called bay), buckeye, and madrone.

Though the majority of redwoods grow on hillsides, our images of the forest come from the smaller areas of flat ground along streams, where the woods are at their most impressive—and their dimmest. A plant that thrives in dense redwood shade is the redwood sorrel, the widespread ground cover that looks, at a glance, like clover. Sorrel is so sun-sensitive that it folds its leaves together like little umbrellas when a beam of direct sunlight chances to fall on it. The plant bears pale pink flowers eight months of the year. Less exclusive to the groves but also especially happy here are many fern species and such broad-leafed, pale-green plants as aralia (elk clover) and western coltsfoot. The versatile California laurel, with its slender, sharply aromatic leaves, does fine in sun but survives in the redwood grove by reaching for available light, growing more sideways than up until it topples over. Former branches then take over as new vertical stems.

Thimbleberry

Over their long history, these big trees have been the changeless element in ever-changing assemblages of plants and animals.

When a redwood or other dominant tree dies or topples, allowing more light to reach the forest floor, the world instantly changes. Many more flowering plants appear, as do the butterflies and other flying insects that pollinate them. Azalea bushes, which flourish in moist spots under the redwoods but barely bloom in the shade, suddenly astonish with their masses of fragrant, creamy, early-summer flowers. Small birds descend for insects, nuts, and seeds. As soon as the opening is created, it begins to fill. Maples spread their broad, light-hungry leaves. Redwood saplings and sprouts shoot upwards, competing to gain height and close the forest canopy again. These evanescent, shifting "lightgaps" are as much a part of the fabric of the forest as the shadows themselves.

Animal life is not very obvious in a redwood forest. During past debates about logging practices (from which Muir Woods was blessedly exempt), timber industry advocates would sometimes speak of "the desert under the trees," suggesting that cutting the redwoods and other old-growth conifers is actually a benefit to wildlife. Much has been learned since about the richness of the animal community in redwood shade.

To grasp the diversity, scientists say, we must look for the inconspicuous invertebrates: the mites, millipedes, isopods, earthworms, snails, slugs, flies, moths, and beetles that break down the abundant dead matter shed by the forest. Most noticeable at Muir Woods are the banana slugs that proliferate in the wet season. Invertebrate communities are quite different from place to place in the redwood region, with many species of extremely local occurrence.

Darner

Buckeye

Painted lady

Echo blue

Pale swallowtail

Pipevine swallowtail

Anglewing

49

Ensatina salamander

Banana slug

When we try to pick out anything by itself, we find it hitched to everything else in the Universe.

John Muir

Redwood logging, biologists surmise, has ended the existence of many small creatures before they were ever described.

The moist green places under redwood trees are habitat for fragile-skinned amphibians, including the rough-skinned newt, the California slender salamander, the Ensatina salamander, and the California giant salamander (it's the color of redwood and barks like a tiny dog). These creatures are easiest to spot in the wet season, in or near quiet stream backwaters, in damp cavities, or under rotting logs or litter.

The most numerous surface-dwelling mammals in Muir Woods are the rodents: gray squirrels, Sonoma chipmunks, valley pocket gophers, deer mice, shrews, dusky-footed woodrats, broad-footed moles, and others. The

Coast range newt

mammals you're most likely to see are hesitant, high-stepping black-tailed deer (perhaps munching on redwood sorrel). The largest predators now are coyotes, bobcats, and gray foxes, with a mountain lion sighted now and again in scrub at the forest's edge. The California grizzly bear is long gone, though a young black bear, on an excursion from more extensive forests in Sonoma County to the north, made headlines by wandering through the neighborhood in 2003. In 2004, a river otter appeared among the redwoods, the first observed in Redwood Creek in three-quarters of a century.

Grey squirrel

Bobcat

Woodrat

Deer mouse

Chipmunk

Coyote

Mountain lion

Pocket gopher

Black-tailed deer

Lady Beetles

On a fall day in Muir Woods, especially on the Bootjack or Fern Creek Trail, you may come across a great mass of orange and black beetles, clinging together on a rock or log. These are the convergent lady beetles, named for the white lines that come together behind the head, though what strikes you first is the handsome pattern of black spots on the glossy, pumpkin-colored wing cases. Known also as ladybugs, the beetles are found all over temperate North America, especially on croplands, where farmers value them as a key control of aphids, a plant pest. In California the beetles hatch in the spring, gorge on aphids through four stages of larval development, and pupate. On emergence from the pupa as adults, the beetles migrate on the wind to cooler sites where they spend as much as nine months in a state of slowed metabolism called estivation, waiting for their prey to become abundant again. In cool temperatures they cluster together for warmth. In late winter the beetles mate and move back to the fields to lay eggs and die.

Sudden Oak Death

In the middle 1990s, something began killing trees in the redwood region. It was near Muir Woods that the disease was first spotted, and the first victims were tanoaks, *Lithocarpus densiflora*, a common but not very prominent species of the redwood belt. But soon the disease turned up in additional places and in other kinds of trees, including the California black oak, the canyon oak, and the handsome and beloved coast live oak, *Quercus agrifolia*.

Because its victims can go from apparently thriving to dead and brown in a matter of weeks, the plague was soon dubbed Sudden Oak Death (SOD). In 2000 the agent, a fungus, was identified and given the name *Phytophthora ramorum*, from roots meaning "infester of twigs." A better name might be "infester of trunks," for the fatal form of the disease attacks in the bole, feeding on the cambium, the vital living layer just under the bark. When the cambium dies in a ring around the bole, water and nutrients cannot reach the upper regions of the tree, which quickly browns and dies. The infection may be present for a couple of years before its dramatic conclusion. (A tree that has time to drop its leaves is afflicted by something else, perhaps insect attack, and has a good chance of recovery.)

In addition to the trees it kills, called "canker hosts," SOD afflicts about a hundred additional species, called "foliar hosts" because the infection stays peripheral and the plants survive. Indeed, it now appears that virtually every species in the forests of coastal California can be affected, from poison oak and huckleberry to the redwoods themselves, though these don't suffer much. Bay laurel, the companion of redwoods in Muir Woods, is thought to be an important SOD host, harboring the fungus without often dying of it.

Where did the oak death come from? It's thought to be something new, either a hybrid of local fungus species or, more probably, a hitchhiker from Asia. Its spores travel in water, getting from tree to tree via streams or in wind-driven rain. Warm, late downpours, which seem to be becoming more frequent in recent years, favor its spread. People inadvertently transmit oak death over longer distances by moving spore-laden mud from place to place on boots and vehicle tires, or in firewood or transplanted plants.

Sudden oak death is changing the look of coastal California. A million trees have already died. On certain hillsides, the brown or barren zones are appalling. And all that dead wood increases the danger of fire on a catastrophic scale.

At Muir Woods, some 90 percent of the tanoaks have now been lost, and the infection is moving into the live oaks on bordering ridges. The effects within the core redwood groves are subtle. Where tanoaks on the forest floor have died, there are numerous new "lightgaps" permitting sunlight to reach the forest floor. Young redwoods, bay laurels, and new oaks are taking advantage of these openings to begin their own reach for the canopy. Among the losers here are acorn eaters like woodpeckers, band-tailed pigeons, and dusky-footed woodrats (main prey species for spotted owls).

There is one treatment that has proved effective on oaks and tanoaks, but nobody is proposing a wholesale inoculation of the woods. Visitors to the forest can help by parking on pavement or gravel, not in mud, and not under bay trees. Especially in the wet season, recreationists are asked to rinse off boots, tires, paws, and hooves before leaving one area for another. The spores are killed by bleach (diluted 10:1 in water), Lysol spray, and alcohol.

The disease may be ultimately curbed by two factors: natural selection and fire. Some individual trees are less susceptible than others; these will have more descendants. Fire kills the spores, and even areas that have burned within the last fifty years are, for unknown reasons, somewhat protected. Nobody wants a wholesale burnoff, but the fungal threat only adds to the urgency of bringing controlled fire back to the woods.

Hoary bat

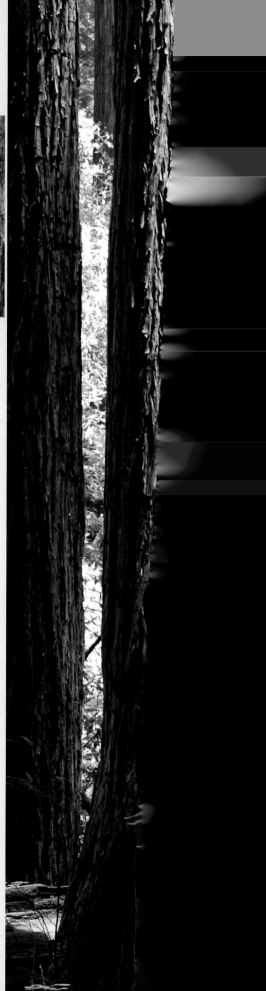

Bats and Birds

Among the animals most tightly linked to the redwoods are winged, warm-blooded ones: the bats, together with certain birds.

Bats like caves, and to a bat a hollow in a big old redwood trunk is as good as a hollow in rock. Ten species have been confirmed in the monument, including the hoary bat, the fringed myotis, and the Mexican free-tailed bat, the species seen swarming by the thousands out of southwestern cave systems like Carlsbad Caverns in New Mexico. Bats roost and breed in Muir Woods, dip down to drink from Redwood Creek, and range out as far as three miles to feed on flying insects. Since most species are on the wing at night and make no noises audible to human ears, the visitor is unlikely to notice the creatures. The bats in their daytime sleep don't seem to take much notice of the visitor, either. It helps that most of the fire-hollows bats favor have formed on the uphill sides of trees, facing away from the

The spotted owl is an "indicator species," representative of all the wild things that live in and depend on complex forests.

heavily traveled valley-bottom trails.

The totem animal of Muir Woods might be the northern spotted owl, *Strix occidentalis caurina*. This is a medium-sized owl, its brown plumage flecked with white. Its eyes are likewise brown, not the usual owl yellow. Its

Owl vs. Owl

Barred owl

The northern spotted owl, the invisible winged icon of Muir Woods, may be in trouble. A similar species called the barred owl, once found only in the eastern United States, has for years been expanding its range westward through Canada and southward along the Pacific Coast. In 2002 it was sighted in Muir Woods, the first observation in Marin County. In 2007 a pair of barred owls raised young in this redwood forest for the first time.

The spotted owl has always shared its world with other owls, but it has never had a competitor like this, at once so similar and so importantly different. The spotted owl eats mostly the dusky-footed woodrat: the barred eats woodrats too but also other prey, including crayfish from Redwood Creek. The spotted owl hunts at night: the barred owl does too but also gathers food by day. The barred resembles the spotted even to the soft brown eyes but is just a bit larger and just a bit more aggressive in competing for the same ecological niche. Park service staff dubbed the first nesting male in Muir Woods "Darth Owl."

Should we worry that one owl threatens to replace another? Should we be intervening in some way? Such displacements are nothing new, though they are happening ever more frequently and quickly in the ecologically unstable world shaped by overwhelming human presence.

People have a lot invested in the spotted owl. As an endangered species, with legal protections, it has been central in the campaign to reform logging practices so that a certain proportion of old forest with big trees is always present. The cause is broad but the tool is so specific as to be rather fragile: must the forest still be protected if the spotted owl is absent?

We see here how the focus on single, imperiled species can both further and distort the case for conservation. As in the old days when conflicts might be decided by a battle of selected champions, the owl has been appointed to represent a whole community, a whole ecosystem.

Olive-sided flycatcher

characteristic call, resembling a very gentle bark, is also quite unlike the classic owl hoot.

The spotted owl is an "indicator species," representative of all the wild things that live in and depend on complex forests. As those forests dwindle, so does this bird. It was declared a threatened species under the federal Endangered Species Act in 1990. Muir Woods has all that the owls need: lofty trees and lesser ones of several kinds; broken tops, snags, and cavities for nesting; open air for flight between the lowest branches and the forest floor; and logs and debris on the ground to house the owls' rodent food (here, the dusky-footed woodrat). Muir Woods marks the limit of the species range, apparently housing the southernmost nesting pair. But lately it has been losing out to its more widespread and aggressive cousin, the barred owl.

Pileated woodpecker

More visible (and audible) to the visitor is the pileated woodpecker, *Dryocopus pileatus*, another large bird at home among large trees. In recent years, a pair has been nesting at Muir Woods in trailside alder snags. The birds are largely black with a bright red crown, larger in the male, and a white underwing that flashes in flight. The pileated makes a noisy drumming as it probes tree bark for insects. The call is a wild, descending laugh. The cartoon character Woody Woodpecker is based on the pileated. The birds excavate a new nest hole each year in a dead, standing tree, leaving ready-made spaces for other cavity nesters whose beaks aren't quite so strong, like the violet-green swallow.

Other birds that raise young at Muir Woods are the Swainson's thrush

Steller's jay

Raven

Snowy egret

and the olive-sided flycatcher, which build their cups on large horizontal branches; the Pacific Slope flycatcher, which favors tree stumps and upturned tree roots; and the Wilson's warbler, which nests in willow thickets. All these birds head south to the tropics for the winter.

Many bird species find conditions at Muir Woods to their liking year-round. You can't miss the bright and noisy Steller's jay, that great talker and scavenger, or the common ravens that patrol the parking lot. Many people notice the Oregon junco and the small but strikingly melodious winter wren, a permanent resident despite its name, busy on the ground along the water. The Anna's hummingbird and the ruby-crowned kinglet, both red-headed,

Winter wren

Belted kingfisher

Swainson's thrush

Wilson's warbler

American goldfinch

are the tiniest birds here but not the hardest to spot. Almost invisible is the little brown creeper, working its way up tree-boles (never down) as it gathers insects.

The creek draws its own particular birds. In the winter, a majestic great blue heron or a smaller, bright-white great egret may wing its way up from the coastline. The egret scrabbles at stream gravels to turn up prey; the heron hunts by stillness, waiting to impale a fish or crustacean with a flash of its sharp bill. From the bank watches the belted kingfisher, with its large, crested head; it hovers and plunges to fish.

All in all, there are 69 bird species in the monument.

Hermit thrush

Varied thrush

Red-tailed hawk

Ravens

Great blue heron

Great horned owlet

Spotted towhee

Scrub jay

White-crowned sparrow

Pacific slope flycatcher

Ruby-crowned kinglet

Oregon junco

Anna's hummingbird

Life in the Water

Large streams in redwood country make corridors through their forests, opening sky. Redwood Creek in Muir Woods is smaller and flows within its forest, its waters cooled by redwood shade and carrying brown redwood needles, yellow redwood pollen, green sprigs blown from the redwood tops above. Like all streams, it is a living space and a highway for many species, from caddis flies to river otters.

The most celebrated creek dwellers are the salmon and steelhead trout that begin their lives among the clean stream gravels. You may not see them, but at whatever time you look, these animals are there: tiny, new-hatched fingerlings; somewhat older fry, their sides spotted and barred with "parr marks" for camouflage; groups of adults returned from the ocean to spawn. Both salmon and steelhead trout are anadromous: they live much of their lives at sea but return to fresh water to reproduce.

Silver or coho salmon, *Oncorhynchus kisutch*, hatch in the spring from tiny orange eggs concealed in the bottom gravel. At first they live off a remnant of egg yolk, still attached; then they feed on small aquatic animals and insects fallen into the stream. They survive the summer drought in lingering pools and threads of water. When the rains come back, they begin making their way down to the sea, reaching it in April or May of their second year. About one in fifty lives to swim in salt water. By then the fish are three to five inches long.

Coho smolts

The salmon spend the next eighteen months at sea, spreading out over much of the western Pacific and mingling with an Asian population of their species. But at the end of that time, they return not only to the correct continent but almost always to the very creek segment in which they were spawned. When the winter rains break the sandbar at Muir Beach, the survivors—twenty-five to one hundred fifty fish—re-enter the stream and labor their way up the current to their natal waters, in and near Muir Woods.

Coho salmon

After some time in fresh water, male coho salmon develop elongated snouts and flanks the color of a fresh-cut redwood log. Females stay silver or turn pinkish, with black spots. Just to glimpse the fish as big red or gray streaks in the current is a thrill. It takes luck and clear water (several days after a rain) to see the moment of spawning: how the female, or hen, digs into the gravel with her tail and deposits eggs, how the male hovers to release milt, how the hen refills the hole and tail-slaps the pebbles to dislodge fine sediment that could cut off vital oxygen. You are more likely on a given winter day to see dilapidated, "spawned out" salmon in eddies, stranded on the bank, or floating off downstream. Like all Pacific Ocean salmon, the coho dies after it reproduces. Salmon carcasses, it is thought, were once an important source of food and fertilizer for streamside forests, though few runs are large enough to contribute much in this way today.

The most celebrated creek dwellers are the salmon and steelhead trout that begin their lives among the clean stream gravels. You may not see them, but at whatever time you look, these animals are there.

72

The trout with the Latin name *Oncorhynchus mykiss* has two common names and two ways of life. Many of the fish live their entire lives in freshwater and are known to anglers as rainbow trout. But where access to the sea is not blocked by dams or other obstacles, the identical fish take on anadromous habits and go by the name steelhead. Redwood Creek steelhead spawn a little later than

Steelhead trout

salmon, and hatch a little later. They may head to the sea after as little as one year or linger in streams for more than two. On return they fight their way a little farther up the local streams. They do not die after one spawning, but instead, make several round trips to the ocean.

Anadromous fish are in trouble these days due to dams that cut off former spawning areas, soil erosion that smothers their spawning gravels in sediment, and overfishing. The coho salmon and steelhead of the central coast of California were listed as "threatened" under the federal Endangered Species Act in 1996 and 1997, and in 2005 the coho was further downgraded to "endangered." At least half the streams of central California have lost their coho salmon entirely. The coho population that comes to Redwood Creek is regarded as especially valuable because it appears to be genetically intact, not contaminated with hatchery-bred salmon, as are the fish in many other streams.

The Uniqueness of Muir Woods

Muir Woods seen as a forest ecosystem is a good deal more remarkable than Muir Woods seen as a collection of individual trees. This stand of redwoods is unusual in being a complete forest, from the central streamside flats where the giants grow to the hilly margins where the grove grades into less regal woods and brushfields. It is also an intact forest: the only sizeable redwood stand near San Francisco Bay that has literally never felt the hand of the logger. Many other redwood parks, grand though they appear, had much wood removed from them in the nineteenth century. Even where the biggest and oldest trees, difficult to bring down with early logging tools, were

spared, younger and smaller generations of trees were severely thinned before protection came. At Muir Woods, the whole natural range is present.

An old-growth redwood forest, by the most comprehensive definition, includes living trees 250 years old or older; younger trees of all ages; dead trees, standing as snags, lying on the ground as logs, and acting as natural dams in streams; thick, multi-layered canopies of branches, needles, and leaves; ground floor plants, including those that flourish in deep shade; diverse appropriate wildlife; and near-natural cycles of stream flooding and forest fire. All of these elements are present at Muir Woods. We must travel far north of San Francisco Bay to find them all in one forest again.

Two

SAVING MUIR WOODS,
AGAIN AND AGAIN

Felling of a *Sequoia
sempervirens, circa
1895–1910*

Muir Woods as we have it today is, in a sense, an accidental treasure.

This forest, for all its massive loveliness, is a rather average specimen of old-growth redwoods in the central part of their range. You won't find here the tallest redwoods, nor the thickest, nor the oldest, nor the lushest woodland floor. Any of a hundred local canyons might equally well have been the site of a first federal redwood park. But, by the late 1800s, those other canyons had all been logged. Human beings, by cutting down all but one of the prominent ancient redwood stands within easy reach of San Francisco, conferred uniqueness on the one they spared.

At that, it was a pretty near thing.

Human beings, by cutting down all but one of the prominent ancient redwood stands within easy reach of San Francisco, conferred uniqueness on the one they spared.

Felled sequoia 25 feet in diameter —circa 1890s, perhaps in Sequoia and Kings Canyon National Parks

Muir Woods, then known as Redwood Canyon, Sequoia Canyon, or Sequoia Valley, survived the logging boom of the middle 1800s by topographical luck. Nestled in their canyon, the trees weren't easily reached from the ridgeline to the east, and the sea cove at the mouth of Redwood Creek was a poor ship's landing. By the 1870s, logging of the canyon had become technically feasible, but owner Samuel Throckmorton chose to defer it, retaining this scenic corner of his vast holdings in southern Marin County as a private hunting and fishing retreat. This policy was continued by the next owner, the Tamalpais Land & Water Company.

Bohemian Club
members sitting
under umbrellas and
enjoying a musical
interlude during
one of the club's
annual midsummer
encampments.

A chance for permanent preservation was missed in the 1890s, when the Bohemian Club came, saw, and shivered. A member of that wealthy fraternity, Henry Gillig, had actually purchased land at the woods on speculation, hoping to resell it to the club for its regular annual encampment. (Gillig built the twisting road down from the ridge that serves the monument to this day.) That September, the club gathered at the spot still called Bohemian Grove to celebrate the annual "Midsummer High Jinks" around a lath-and-plaster Buddha seventy feet high. But the following night under fog-wet canvas was cold enough, club records state, to "freeze the male evidence off a brass monkey." At a meeting later that fall, the members declined to accept the site, and the parcel reverted to the Land & Water Company.

Ten years later, logging appeared imminent.

William Kent, 1913

William Kent's Woods

Enter the person for whom Muir Woods is notably not named, William Kent. A man of ambition, conscience, and wealth, Kent had large plans for the Mount Tamalpais region. As the owner of extensive lands there, he hoped to profit from the tourist trade. As a conservationist, he wanted to see founded on the mountain a national park "on the lines of Yellowstone." As a member of the hunting club that frequented the future Muir Woods, he knew Sequoia Canyon well and saw it as central to the big park plan.

In 1903, at a meeting in Mill Valley, Kent called into being a Mount Tamalpais National Park Association. Among those present was Gifford Pinchot, the great founding figure of American forestry. Almost instantly there came a query from a sympathizer at the Land & Water Company: Would Kent himself buy these redwoods to save them from the saw?

> *"If we lost all the money we have and saved these trees, it would be worthwhile, wouldn't it?"*

Kent's fortune consisted largely of unprofitable landholdings, and the economy at the moment wasn't good. "I informed him that I could not afford to own any more white elephants, and wanted to know why the . . . Company did not preserve [the trees] themselves."

But Kent found himself unable to walk away. "The beauty of the place attracted me, and got on my mind, and I could not forget the situation." Finally, in 1905, he plunged, purchasing 611 acres for the discounted but still-formidable sum of $45,000. His wife, Elizabeth Thacher Kent, recalls the answer she got when she questioned the expense: "If we lost all the money we have and saved these trees, it would be worthwhile, wouldn't it?" Kent may just have meant it. Later, only half-joking, he would use similar words to urge a California governor to buy additional redwood parks at any cost: "Damn the public schools, Bill! Shut them up for a year and save those trees!"

One year after Kent acquired his forest, San Francisco lay in ashes in the aftermath of earthquake and fire, waiting to be built all over again with redwood lumber. But none of that lumber, now, would come from Sequoia Canyon.

Muir Woods, 1915

Circa 1900

Kent hoped to get his money back by making the grove a rustic private resort. Along with his father, he was one of the backers of a tourist railroad that then climbed from Mill Valley to the summit of Mount Tamalpais. He struck a deal with the operators: If they would build a branch line down to the upper edge of the woods, he would construct a hotel and lease the whole canyon to the railroad for an annual rent and a share of the ticket sales.

But other interests were eying the valley of the trees. On December 2, 1907, while the Kents were away on vacation, a local water company filed suit to acquire land in the heart of the woods for a dam and reservoir. As the provider of a public service, the company had the right to force the sale. Returning the next day, Kent telegraphed Pinchot, now head of the United States Forest Service in Washington, D.C.:

TOP: Original Muir Woods Inn
BOTTOM: Postcard, circa 1913

CONDEMNATION AND DESTRUCTION OF REDWOOD CAÑON THREATENED BY WATER COMPANY. MUST HAVE IT ACCEPTED AS NATIONAL FOREST AT ONCE.... SOLE IDEA IS TO SAVE TREES FOR PUBLIC. WIRE ACCEPTANCE AND TERMS. VITALLY URGENT. ANSWER KENTFIELD, MARIN COUNTY, CALIFORNIA.

It was not as a forest reserve, however, that the tract would enter the public domain. Kent soon got wind of a uniquely appropriate tool: the Antiquities Act of 1906. This novel law allowed the president, acting alone, to set aside areas of federally owned land as untouchable national monuments, similar to national parks but needing no Congressional approval.

Martinez, Feb. 6, 1908.

Dear Mr Kent,

Seeing my name in
the tender & deed of the Tamalpais
Sequoias was a surprise of the
pleasantest kind. This is the
best tree-lover's monument that
could possibly be found in all
the forests of the world. You
have done me great honor, &
I am proud of it. Schools here
& there have planted "Muir trees" in their
playgrounds, & long ago Asa Gray
named several plants for me, the
most interesting of which is a sturdy
frost-enduring daisy that I discover
on the shore of the Arctic Ocean near
Icy Cape; a Sierra peak also & one of
the Alaska glaciers bear my name
but these aboriginal woods, barring
human action, will outlast them
all, even the mountain & glacier.
Compared with Sequoia glaciers are
young fleeting things, & since the
first Sequoia forests lifted their

domes & spires to the sky, mounta
great & small, thousands of them,
have been weathered, ground down,
washed away & cast into the sea;
while two of the many species
of Sequoia have come safely
through all the geological changes
& storms that have fallen upon
them since Cretaceous times,
surviving even the crushing
destroying ice-sheets of the
Glacial Period.
Saving these woods from the axe
& saw, from money-changers &
water changers, & giving them
to our country & the world is
in many ways the most notable
service to God & man I've heard
of since my forest wanderings
began. a much needed lesson
& blessing to saint & sinner alike.
& credit & encouragement to God.
That so fine divine a thing should
have come out of money-mad Chicago!
Wha wad a' thocht it! Immortal Sequoia
life to you. Ever Yours, John Muir

John Muir and William Kent at the Muir Woods Inn, 1910

Gift to the Nation

As Christmas approached, Kent bombarded Washington with letters, photographs, and articles about Redwood Canyon; Pinchot took the case to President Theodore Roosevelt. Things moved. On New Year's Eve, Interior Secretary James R. Garfield signed the deed accepting Kent's gift to the nation of 298 acres, including the entire old-growth redwood forest. On January 9, 1908, one day before the condemnation axe had been due to fall, the president declared the land a national monument, inviolable. In a public exchange of letters, the president urged that the monument be named Kent Woods, for the donor; but Kent insisted that it bear instead the name of prominent conservationist John Muir. Muir accepted in solemn phrases, describing the gift as a "credit and encouragement to God."

Muir Woods, the tenth area Teddy Roosevelt set aside under the Antiquities Act, was in several ways a first. It was the first monument whose major attraction was a living thing rather than something like an archeological site. It was also the first federal park created on donated private land, and the first such park in close proximity to a city: important precedents, all.

His great gift to the people did not end Kent's connection with Muir Woods. He still owned much land around the central groves, including the monument's parking lot and the springs that gave it drinking water. For a number of years after the donation, Kent paid a caretaker to run the property. Even when the government finally took up that burden, the caretaker was "Kent's man."

From 1911 to 1918, Kent served in Congress, where he advocated creation of a large Redwood National Park in far northern California, an idea it would take another fifty years to realize. He also was a prime mover behind the 1916 law creating the National Park Service to manage the nation's most precious natural treasures, including Muir Woods. Back home in the 1920s, he plugged away on his project of blanketing Mount Tamalpais with public land. He himself gave additional acreage to the national monument; to the Marin Municipal Water District that he had helped to found; and, just before his death in 1928, to the new Mount Tamalpais State Park, adjoining the monument on the northern, uphill side.

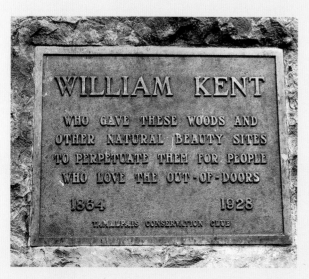

William Kent is memorialized at only one spot in Muir Woods: up the canyon of Fern Creek, on a plaque on a rock beside the log of an enormous Douglas-fir. Volunteers from the Tamalpais Conservation Club placed this monument in 1929. This tree, Kent's favorite, was once taller than any of the monument's redwoods. In the winter of 1981–82, a storm tore off the top of the fir. In 2003, the giant fell. A redwood, you can't help thinking, would be flourishing yet.

January 22, 1908.

My dear Mr. Kent:

I have just received from Secretary Garfield your very generous letter enclosing the gift of Redwood Canyon to the National Government to be kept as a perpetual park for the preservation of the giant redwoods therein and to be named the Muir National Monument.   You have doubtless seen my proclamation of January 9th, instant, creating this monument.   I thank you most heartily for this singularly generous and public spirited action on your part.   All Americans who prize the natural beauties of the country and wish to see them preserved undamaged, and especially those who realize the literally unique value of the groves of giant trees, must feel that you have conferred a great and lasting benefit upon the whole country.

I have a very great admiration for John Muir; but after all, my dear sir, this is your gift.   No other land than that which you give is included in this tract of nearly 300 acres and I should greatly like to name the monument the Kent Monument if you will permit it.

Sincerely yours,

Theodore Roosevelt

Namesake John Muir

One Muir Woods visitor very sensibly asks: "What's a Muir?"

John Muir. 1838–1914. Scientist, farmer, inventor, adventurer, canny businessman: but above all, American conservationist. Born in Scotland, raised in Wisconsin. Reborn, he said, in 1867, when a factory accident left him temporarily blind.

Lying in darkness, Muir made a promise to himself: if his sight came back, he would work at a trade no more but would spend the rest of his life exploring the bright world. "I might have become a millionaire," he wrote. "I chose to become a tramp." His wanderings would indeed be prodigious, but one place above all was to become his spiritual home: the Yosemite country in California's Sierra Nevada Range.

Wherever Muir went, he saw the American landscape being abused, especially by brutal overgrazing, uncontrolled logging, and rapacious mining practices. His anger grew, and he began to write.

After an interlude in which he started a family and grumblingly but profitably raised fruit in Martinez, California, Muir made conservation his full-time career. His increasingly eloquent nature articles and polemics appeared in every influential journal. He argued and lobbied and pleaded and pressured and fought. And people listened. Largely due to his work, Yosemite became a national park in 1890.

In 1892, Muir became the first president of the Sierra Club. With the club, he saw millions of acres of public land become national parks and national forests. And he kept on writing. By the time Muir Woods was named for him in 1908, John Muir had helped to create a whole new climate of opinion.

Muir's involvement with his namesake grove was peripheral. In 1903, when the centennial of Ralph Waldo Emerson's birth was observed among the trees, he sent a message but did not attend. Apparently he visited in 1904, in the company of Gifford Pinchot but not of Kent, who even then, a contemporary letter shows, contemplated naming the woods for him. Muir and Kent definitely toured together in 1908. At that point each regarded the other as an ally.

John Muir, 1907

President Theodore Roosevelt and John Muir at Yosemite, 1903

Climb the mountains and get their good tidings. Nature's peace will flow into you as sunshine flows into trees. The winds will blow their freshness into you, and the storms their energy, while cares will drop off like autumn leaves.

John Muir

Pinchot tree circa 1925–1930

Leaders at Odds

Muir's worst defeat came at the place he cared about most of all. In 1913, Congress voted to let the City of San Francisco invade Yosemite National Park and build a dam on the Tuolumne River, drowning the superlative gorge called Hetch Hetchy, "the other Yosemite Valley." Among the voices for that dam was Gifford Pinchot; among the votes for it was Congressman William Kent, the savior of Redwood Creek six years before. In taking this stand, Kent was promoting another cause of his: government rather than private ownership of key water and electricity supplies.

The bitter Hetch Hetchy debate helped to convince all sides that there needed to be a law defining the uses of parks and creating, for the first time, a special office to manage places like Muir Woods and Yosemite—the National Park Service. The man who introduced the National Park Service Organic Act of 1916: William Kent.

Puzzling? Ironic? Neither, really. However simple the conservation issues of the early 1900s look in hindsight—however clearly we may think we see who was right, wrong, or inconsistent—they were not simple then. It was a time when foundations were being laid. The people who laid them often disagreed.

There is at Muir Woods a great tree dedicated to Gifford Pinchot, without whose help, indeed, it might no longer stand. The Sierra Club placed a plaque at its base in 1910. William Kent served lunch. Pinchot was not present. He was unhappy that Muir Woods had not been given to his Forest Service for management. Muir was not present. He disliked Pinchot as a man who saw forests only as sources of lumber and other commercial values.

Kent, Muir, Pinchot: Muir Woods needed them all.

Theodore Roosevelt (left) and
Gifford Pinchot (right), 1907

William Kent (left) and first National Park Service director
Stephen T. Mather (right) at the Pinchot Tree, 1923

This grand show is eternal. It is always sunrise somewhere; the dew is never all dried at once; a shower is forever falling; vapor is ever rising. Eternal sunrise, eternal sunset, eternal dawn and gloaming, on sea and continents and islands, each in its turn, as the round earth rolls.

John Muir

Laura Lyon White and Elizabeth Thacher Kent

At a key moment in the story of Muir Woods, banker Lovell White agreed to sell the property to William Kent. But not so fast, gentlemen: the name Elizabeth Thacher Kent was also on that deed, and Laura Lyon White, the banker's wife, may have held the secret key to the transaction.

The saving of Muir Woods happened near the high point of the Progressive Movement, the diffuse but powerful reaction to the social ills of the era following the Civil War. Conservation was one of the big Progressive themes. So were planning and the creation of more livable cities. So was women's suffrage—the extension of the right to vote—a movement in which both Mrs. Kent and Mrs. White at different times were active.

Born in Indiana in 1839, Laura Lyon attended Oberlin College when it was somewhat scandalous for a woman to pursue higher education. In 1859, she came west with her husband to live in a rough California mining town, where she bore and lost two children. In 1864, the couple moved to San Francisco. Like many wealthy city dwellers, they also acquired a hilltop summer home in Mill Valley, one ridge over from what would become Muir Woods.

Lovell desperately wanted to try again for a son and heir: Laura, apparently, wasn't so sure. Her biography hints at the striking of a bargain of sorts. In any case, after the birth of son Ralston in 1877, Lovell became a loyal supporter, financially and otherwise, of Laura's charitable causes. At about the same time, Laura turned away from an early interest in the campaign for the vote, choosing instead to put her energy into areas the time deemed the ideal province of her sex: small matters such as education, prison reform, and the preservation of natural beauty.

Laura Lyon White

Elizabeth Kent with her son Albert, circa 1891

In 1897, Laura founded the influential California Club, which among other things campaigned to preserve the giant sequoias at what is now Calaveras Big Trees State Park. In 1903, she became president of the Sempervirens Club, which was working to protect the coast redwoods at Big Basin south of San Francisco. In 1904, when the redwoods at Muir Woods were up for grabs, the California Club launched a public campaign to protect the site. The private channel may have been more important, for the owner of the property, the Tamalpais Land & Water Company, was headed up by none other than her husband Lovell White.

On the other side of the transaction, the traditional account has William Kent persuading his reluctant spouse to go along, but one wonders how hard that was. Elizabeth Thacher Kent was herself a full-blooded Progressive and probably shared her husband's conservation bent. When William went to Congress, she became prominent in the women's suffrage movement. In spring of 1917, she was among the activists who picketed Woodrow Wilson's White House for the cause. After the passage of the suffrage amendment in 1920, she continued working on peace and social justice issues until her death in 1952.

Manzanita

Alice Eastwood

On the morning of April 6, 1906, in the moment of shock between two disasters, a woman named Alice Eastwood was making her way into the ruinous building that had housed the California Academy of Sciences. She wanted to get to the sixth floor. The spiral staircase was in rubble, but its metal railing was intact, and it was up that shaky path that Eastwood clambered her way.

The great San Francisco earthquake was over—the ensuing and even more catastrophic fire still to come. Eastwood, the academy's curator of botany, was risking her life to save the precious "type collection," the assemblage of plant samples on which plant description and nomenclature in this part of the world were based.

Eastwood's spryness would have come as no surprise to fellow botanists who tried to keep up with her on the trails of Mount Tamalpais. Besides her city home on Russian Hill, Eastwood had a cabin in Mill Valley, knew every corner of southern Marin, and contributed much to knowledge of the region.

Miner's lettuce

Star lily

Of course she was a friend of William and Elizabeth Kent. She met and influenced Kent's cousin, Mary Elizabeth Parsons, author of the pioneering 1897 book *The Wildflowers of California*. In 1904, she toasted the Kents' pending acquisition of the woods at a Thanksgiving picnic in the grove. In 1912, she helped William found the Tamalpais Conservation Club to pursue his larger preservation goals.

When Eastwood's summer place burned down in a forest fire, her attention went less to her loss than to the plants on the blackened hillside: what died, what recovered, and what surprisingly flourished. In an article titled "The Aftergrowth of a Mountain Fire," she noted that the roots of the manzanita and California lilac resprouted after the flames. "Stranger than the behavior of these woody plants," she wrote, "is that of some of the humble herbs. These appear for a year or two, then are not seen again until another fire when once again they spring forth." It was one of the first shrewd observations about the natural role of fire.

In her more than fifty years as curator at the academy, the pioneering botanist received many honors. Two of the best came very late. In 1949, on the occasion of her retirement, the state park campground just above Muir Woods, former terminus of the Muir Woods and Mount Tamalpais Scenic Railroad, was renamed Camp Alice Eastwood. The following year, she traveled to Sweden for the 7th International Botanical Congress, where she served as honorary president and was enthroned in a chair used by Linnaeus, the founder of modern taxonomy. She died in 1953 at the age of ninety-five.

Inn - Muir Woods
MT. TAMALPAIS & MUIR WOODS R
CALIFORNIA.

Opening the Woods

Today the front door of Muir Woods is the southern, downstream end. But from its beginnings to 1929, the park faced the other way. Most visitors came from the north, over the flank of the mountain, and most came either on foot or on the Mount Tamalpais and Muir Woods Railway.

In service since 1892, this famous railway line steamed from Mill Valley all the way up the local mountain, mounting 2,300 feet on a route whose magnificent kinkiness made it "The Crookedest Railroad in the World." In 1907, the line sent a branch down toward the new Muir Woods National Monument. Its original terminus was a flat area north of the monument boundary, now known as Camp Alice Eastwood, where stood the Muir or Muir Woods Inn; a carriage road, used as a broad trail today, linked down to the redwoods.

Some of the trains that ran down to the inn were unpowered "gravity cars." Passengers loved these descents, the almost silent, effortless passages down slopes sleek with chaparral, watching the tips of the great trees rise toward them. The trips back up, of course, required laboring engines.

Scenic Railway. Mount Tamalpais, California.

5059. *Through the Redwood forest. Mt. Tamalpais Scenic Railway approaching Mt. Tamalpais.*

After the first inn burned down in 1913, the railroad line was pushed nearer the valley floor and a second Muir Inn constructed. Paths and stairs led down to the redwoods. To see the second inn site, you can walk a few hundred yards up from the valley floor on the old carriage road, following signs to Camp Alice Eastwood; the inn stood at a gentle bend just beyond the second sharp switchback. The railroad grade, heavily overgrown, parallels the carriage road on a high alignment, crossing it near the notch called the Plevin Cut.

People who didn't come by rail, if old statistics can be believed, came largely on foot; but auto travel soon was important, too. The first car, a Winton, rattled down from the ridge in the winter of 1907–08 on the old Bohemian Club road. William Kent was the reluctant owner of that route, which the government declined to take off his hands. To offset the expense of maintaining it, Kent finally began collecting tolls.

In 1929, an extensive fire burned on Tamalpais. One fire-fighting crew, nearly trapped by the flames, escaped to Muir Woods Inn on the gravity car. But the Muir Woods branch never saw another train, and the whole railway soon shut down for good, due less to fire damage than to the ascendancy of the private automobile. The orphaned inn was torn down in 1932. Lumber and fittings wound up in several unobtrusive park buildings.

LEFT TOP: Postcard of the Mt. Tamalpais Scenic Railway, circa 1908
LEFT BOTTOM: Gravity car

ABOVE: Mount Tamalpais Railroad excursion into Muir Woods, 1927

American Federation of Labor group
luncheon in Muir Woods, 1934

The Little Shop in the Woods
Muir Woods National Monument

Looking upward
among the Redwood

The National Park Service
at Muir Woods

The 1916 Act of Congress establishing the National Park Service told the new agency to do two things in its domains: first, "to conserve the scenery and the natural and historic objects and the wildlife therein" and, second, "to provide for the enjoyment of the same."

It had occurred to no one yet that conservation and enjoyment might sometimes pull against each other—that it takes hard and intelligent work to conserve what large numbers of people come to enjoy. The tiny and hugely popular park called Muir Woods National Monument would quickly prove the point.

Early in its career as a park, Muir Woods was an open place, welcoming, sometimes crowded, with every comfort available under the big red trees and no one to tell you not to trample the moss. At one time you could take your car clear through it. There were as many as sixteen footbridges across the creek (compare the current four). Picnic tables and restrooms stood everywhere among the trees. Groups of several hundred sang songs around great bonfires.

There was a price.

As early as the 1920s, it became apparent that the web and texture of the forest floor were fraying. Where ferns had been, and all the wide-leafed, subtly flowering things, now were trampled paths and swatches of bare dirt. Erosion was uncovering redwood roots. The distressed trees were sprouting from basal burls, but nobody noticed, for the traffic stripped the new shoots off as fast as they appeared. There was also wholesale "poaching" of such valued plants as ferns and trilliums. The five-finger ferns that had lined the creekbank disappeared entirely.

Muir Woods
concession, 1936

National Park Service files tell a repeated story of alarm, attempted corrective action, cautious optimism, and alarm renewed. In 1923, at William Kent's behest, the road through the grove was closed to cars. Overnight camping was curtailed in 1924. The 1929 demise of the Mount Tamalpais and Muir Woods Railway took some of the foot traffic out of the upper groves—and shifted it to the lower ones. In 1933, campfires were banned within the monument. J. Barton Herschler, Monument Custodian during that decade, forbade ballgames in the groves and was "most vigilant in apprehending fern-pickers and initial-carvers." In the late '30s, though, when the Golden Gate Bridge opened and the tollgates were taken off the Muir Woods road, use abruptly tripled, accelerating the wear and tear.

At the same time, the park was energetically pursuing some policies that we now know to have been misguided. In the 1930s, Redwood Creek was almost completely channelized between rock revetments and carefully cleaned of litter and down wood. The forest floor, too, was maintained like a city park. Wildfire continued to be strictly suppressed. The natural values that

were supposed to be sacrosanct were in fact under manifold pressure, from well-meaning managers no less than from careless visitors.

Ranger force on duty during the Golden Gate Bridge Fiesta, June 1937

The next attempt to rebalance use and preservation came in the 1950s. After years of discussion, the last of the picnic tables that had stood in many spots among the trees were removed. In the same decade, the excess bridges across Redwood Creek came down. The park also pulled out the signs that had made special attractions of the tallest tree and others that were notable or curious. Each tree had been the center of a trampled zone and, indeed, the object of a certain amount of vandalism.

Rangers made it a project to rebuild groundcover. Visiting side canyons, they carried down cuttings and seedlings. They brought down sword fern, the characteristic low plant of the woods, with its stiff green angular fronds. They transplanted *Woodwardia fimbriata*, the intricate giant chain fern. Planted five-finger fern on denuded creekbanks. Coaxed redwood sorrel over barren ground. This process has continued ever since.

NPS management training class, 1941

WOODS
MONUMENT
~ DEPARTMENT OF INTERIOR

The CCC at Muir Woods

People come to Muir Woods for nature, but they park and walk on pavements, eat and buy books under roofs, hike and run on carefully constructed trails. The park is in part an artificial landscape. Much of that artifice reflects the work of the New Deal army called the Civilian Conservation Corps.

The CCC, first known as Emergency Conservation Work, was founded in the spring of 1933 to employ young men between the ages of seventeen and twenty-eight for six-month, renewable stints. If its first purpose was to provide jobs, its second was to do good things in national parks, state parks, and government-owned forests. And its army of labor—over half a million, at the peak—indeed changed the face of the public lands.

Things happened fast in those desperate days. President Franklin Delano Roosevelt took the oath of office on March 4, 1933. The CCC law passed on March 31. By the end of June, there were 270,000 young men at work out of 1,330 camps around the country. The hub in Marin County was the site now known as Camp Alice Eastwood, just outside the monument boundary. The following year, reported monument custodian J. Barton Herschler, was "the greatest period of development ever experienced in Muir Woods."

Within the monument, the laborers built several structures in a distinctive yet deliberately restrained style that has come to be known as National Park Rustic. The idea, novel at the time, was to build with nature, on an unobtrusive scale, using local materials like hand-hewn timbers and stone. You have to know just

Temporary quarters, first CCC camp, Lake Lagunitas, 1933

where to look at Muir Woods to find the old CCC work, but the style established then has been consciously continued in every more recent building, bench, bridge, fence, and sign. Elsewhere on the mountain, CCC labor built the fire lookout on the East Peak of Tamalpais and the open-air Cushman Amphitheatre, modeled on a Greek theater and located at the very springs of Redwood Creek; it is the site of an annual Mountain Play. The CCC also laid out or improved many miles of local trails.

This garage was completed in May 1931, illustrating exposed timber framing detail

In June of 1942, against the wishes of the president, Congress abolished the Civilian Conservation Corps.

Much of the legacy of the CCC has faded. Old forestry maps in many regions show whole trail networks blazed by the CCC, left untended in later decades, and long since overgrown or gobbled up by logging roads. But the buildings of that era—those brown-painted, rough-hewn structures that seem to grow out of the ground—still provide our image of what architecture in parks and forests should be. And in a time when every agency that manages public land is underfunded and understaffed, it is hard to avoid a pang of nostalgia for a time when as many as half a million pairs of willing hands were in the woods, doing whatever needed to be done.

The Return of the Woods

Despite all these efforts, Muir Woods was slow to lose its sad and trampled look. Increased visitation (up to 784,000 by 1967) largely swamped the restoration work. Meanwhile, national attitudes were changing. People were taking a fresh look at the national park idea. Critics pointed out that the 1916 act did not, in truth, put recreation on an equal footing with protection of nature: parks are to be made available for public enjoyment "in such a manner and by such means as will leave them unimpaired for the enjoyment of future generations." Despite decades of diligence, Muir Woods was failing this test.

Plainly, if the park was to welcome its ever-increasing public, the style of the welcome would have to undergo a further change. What had begun as a playground would have to complete its evolution into something more jealously cherished, a living museum for redwoods and the species that flourish among and with them.

In 1968, Muir Woods began a process of limiting its trails. Where people had wandered among the trees, now there were defined paths, lined with substantial split-rail fences and—to protect the shallow-lying redwood roots—surfaced with asphalt. It was paradoxical but unavoidable: to better protect this example of the forest primeval, bits of it had to be paved.

The results could be seen about a mile into the monument in the redwood cluster called Cathedral Grove, where the trail splits around an island of big red trunks. Until 1971, those pillars stood in a desert of trampled ground. Then the fences went up. By the following May, new redwood shoots were appearing: "probably the first permitted to develop to this visible stage in seventy years," the superintendent reported. Rangers planted redwood seedlings on the island, too, and dozens of ferns. This time, protected behind fences, the new plants took hold. This spot, like a dozen other former wastelands in Muir Woods, soon looked aboriginal.

It took a few more years to take the next step: to break the long-established habit of housekeeping—keeping the forest floor tidy, free of straggling branches and brushy deadfalls. Yet it was no secret that debris builds soil, feeds insects, draws birds. Salamanders, shrews, the woodrats that feed the owls, all need low-lying "clutter." Finally, about 1980, the automatic cleanup ceased. Now, unless there's a specific reason for removing them, things that fall in the forest are left to lie.

The new untidiness may spoil a few photographic compositions. But to a naturalist's eye, Muir Woods today is looking better and working better than it has for the larger part of a century. The old, bare, stingy look is long gone. There seem to be more flowers, more insects, more warblers, woodpeckers, wrens. Azalea and rhododendron have multiplied. Some characteristic plants that had all but disappeared—minty yerba buena, for example, and wild ginger with its curious brown three-tendril flower—have regained their places in the natural garden.

Other plants have had to be discouraged. Muir Woods is close to urban neighborhoods and former ranches, and from these have spread species alien to the natural fabric of the woods. Down from the site of the Muir Woods Inn came the tough and pretty forget-me-not, named for its hooked, cuff-clinging seed, competing with the native redwood sorrel. From the ridge to the east came the virulent French and Scotch broom, thickets of which now spread over large acreages in Marin County. Himalayan blackberry, poison hemlock, star thistle, pampas grass: the list of undesirables goes on and on. So does the process of pulling out the invaders. The central groves, at least, are now nearly free of them.

Muir Woods still has to be called a recovering forest. But year by year, it seems to be fuller of that green and lively light, shady yet somehow never dim, that the dusty eye takes in as a thirsty throat takes in water.

California rhododendron

Lady fern

Wild ginger

Yerba buena

Refining the Art

The "saving" of Muir Woods, its preservation and restoration as an island of ecological normality in what is in many ways a ravaged world, is a process that has no end. In the new millennium, its managers are learning of new aspects that require attention, and finding new and subtler tools for the task.

However necessary, the paved paths of the 1970s are a discord in the natural scene. Beginning in 1999, several hundred yards at two locations were replaced with raised boardwalks, uncovering the soil beneath and allowing visitors to get a little closer to the trees. Built of recycled redwood lumber, the walkways are narrower than the former paths, without handrails, and deliberately though slightly irregular. In the future, these may be extended. There are plans to shift other trails farther away from the creek, giving streamside vegetation more room to thrive.

The regeneration of the forest floor, natural and human-assisted, proceeds. Instead of robbing remote parts of the forest, however, the park now draws on a native plant nursery, located just downstream from the overflow parking lot. Every Earth Day, hundreds of volunteers plant a thousand or more seedlings.

In recent years, attention has turned to an invisible intruder: human-caused noise. Since 2002, volunteers have been cataloging the sounds heard during day and night and noting how often the subtle messages of the woods—wind, water, birdcalls—are upstaged by loud voices, banging trash bin lids, cell phones, distant airplanes. A survey found that visitors preferred the natural woodland sounds to their own. If owls and bats could be surveyed, they would probably concur. Signs now encourage visitors to talk quietly, turn off phones, and close bins carefully. Buttons and stickers are available: "Smile . . . if you are listening to the forest!"

The park schedules a quiet period at midday, and in 2006, Cathedral Grove was designated a "Quiet Zone," an experiment made permanent in honor of the park's 2008 centennial. The National Park Service is also asking the Federal Aviation Administration to create a no-fly zone above the monument in order to reduce the sometimes penetrating noise of small planes.

Like too much sound, too much light can be a problem in the woods, disturbing both creatures that sleep at night and those that hunt or forage in the dark hours. In recent years, night lighting has been curbed and necessary emergency lighting dimmed or shielded.

Muir Woods a Century On

What would John Muir think today if he saw the woods that bear his name, one hundred years after they were saved from the saws? Certainly, he wouldn't confuse the place with the true wild places that he loved. Fenced, paved, interpreted, this park is in some ways far from natural. It has even been dismissed as a "zoo for trees."

Yet the zoo comparison is almost an inversion of the truth. In a zoo, people circulate among animals that are confined and far from their native places. Here, the forest is where it always was. It is the human visitors who, for the sake of the trees, agree to confine themselves.

And if this is not a vast, primitive park, not really a place to grasp "the freedom of the hills," it has another function. It is a contact point, a place of meeting. For many millions of visitors, it is the first redwood grove they have seen. For many more, it is the first encounter with the national park idea: that there are places where the preservation of an ecosystem—down to the last tree, shrub, shrew, newt, fish, fungus, and owl—is paramount. Both the trees and the idea, in truth, take a little getting used to.

William Kent, we remember, once urged the governor to close schools and save forests. He didn't go on to observe that forests can also be schools. John Muir would have made much of that point, had he been in on the exchange.

If Muir visited his woods today? He probably wouldn't care much for the parking lot. Once past that and homing into the green, watching the people watch the trees, hearing in unknown languages the upward lilt of awe, I suspect he would declare himself well pleased.

This is the best tree-lover's monument that could possibly be found in all the forests of the world.

John Muir

Three

MUIR WOODS IN
THE WORLD

Muir Woods is in good hands, but it is not a safely isolated world.

It is a little piece of land on one slope of a mountain, in the middle reach of a minor stream valley, on the fringe of a rapidly growing urban region. It is a node in natural networks extending tens, hundreds, or thousands of miles outside its boundaries. Some of its birds winter in the tropics. Even its bats and owls hunt in territories several times the monument's size. Its health depends, ultimately, on ocean currents, climate, and events on a planetary scale.

Most immediately, Muir Woods is part of a stream drainage or watershed, affected by the higher land from which rainfall runs into it: affected also, through its lifeline creek, by all the land downstream. The same good luck and human dedication that saved the forest itself have worked over the years to protect this most intimate frame.

Dias Ridge Trail overlooking Muir Beach

The Watershed

There are, according to the U.S. Geological Survey, twenty-two streams in California named Redwood Creek. The Redwood Creek that drains the bony flank of Mount Tamalpais and passes through Muir Woods on its course to the sea, three miles below the big trees, is among the smallest: six miles long in all, and receiving water from a basin of just nine square miles. It is nonetheless a jewel among the Redwood Creeks because it is in such good shape, relatively speaking. It is free of dams and major water diversions; its waters are clear and cool; it has, more or less, the bugs and birds and fish that it ought to have.

A three-dimensional model of the watershed is the centerpiece of the visitor center where perhaps you have purchased this book. Better than words, it shows the three faces of this valley. Farthest up, on the chaparral-covered steeps of Mount Tamalpais, small, seasonal streams form in several ravines and flow south and a bit eastward. On the way down, they coalesce into two year-round streams, Fern Creek on the east and Redwood Creek on the west. The two join up just inside the national monument boundary (the reservoir plan of 1907 would have placed a dam below this junction). For the next two miles, the combined stream flows southeastward among the redwoods in a sun-sheltered, wind-sheltered valley.

Then, at the monument entrance, stream and valley make an abrupt right turn toward the coast, into the coastal breezes and the afternoon sun. In this segment, called Franks Valley, oaks and bays and wind-pruned buckeyes cloak the land, with willows and alders along the creek and grassy or brushy openings on the ridges. Kent Canyon enters on the right; this fold in the land, topographically shady and wind-sheltered, supports its own redwood stand.

In its lower course, Redwood Creek curves gradually southward and then sharply west again to the sea, where it pools in summer behind coastal dunes. This cove is the spot in the watershed where people have always lived. The Miwok people had their local village here, and the modern community of Muir Beach, population 295, is probably not dissimilar in size. Just before the mouth, a final tributary, Green Gulch Creek, joins in from the left-hand side.

The Greening of Redwood Creek

In his plan for a Mount Tamalpais National Park, William Kent already understood the importance of protecting at least the land above the redwood grove. In 1911, he helped create the Marin Municipal Water District, which acquired the upper slopes of Tamalpais from a local water company. A privately owned strip remained between the upper edge of Muir Woods and the lower edge of the district land. In the 1920s, plans were floated for a new road traversing that strip, the future Panoramic Highway. Knowing that landowners along the route planned to subdivide, conservationists opposed construction. In a compromise, the road was built, but the area it traversed was incorporated into a new Mount Tamalpais State Park, to which Kent gave some acreage just before his death. The "high country" above the redwoods was now secure.

Nothing along Redwood Creek speaks so loudly for joint action as the health of the creek itself, with its small and threatened populations of coho salmon and steelhead trout.

The next act in the preservation of the Redwood Creek watershed opened twenty years later, when a young San Francisco physician named Edgar Wayburn came back from World War II and returned to his old haunts on Bay Area trails, especially those on Mount Tamalpais. Seeing how rapidly suburbs were covering the surrounding countryside, he became involved, through the Sierra Club, in efforts to preserve key lands. Wayburn wondered if the dairy ranches along lower Redwood Creek, farmed for generations by dairymen of Portuguese extraction, would be up for development next. "Don't worry," he was told. "These people have been here forever and will always keep their ranches." Wayburn wasn't so sure.

One summer day in 1947, walking a hillside above Muir Woods near the Ocean View Trail, Wayburn looked out over the shaggy treetops and the valley below and grasped what it was here that needed preserving: not this parcel or that, but the entire drainage basin of Redwood Creek, from bordering ridgeline to bordering ridgeline and from mountain peak to salt water.

A few months later, he learned that the big Dias Ranch, adjoining the national monument downstream in the stretch called Franks Valley, had been sold to speculators. "That really got me going." Making contact with the new owners, Wayburn found them unexpectedly receptive, willing to hold off development while conservationists pushed the state to buy the land. The California Department of Parks and Recreation, on the other hand, proved

Circa 1933

skeptical. It didn't help that thick fog swirled in the canyon on the day when top officials first came to check out the view. Only in 1955, after seven years of lobbying, testimony, and continuing landowner patience, did the legislature agree to purchase the Dias Ranch, and it took yet another five years for the land to be acquired.

In 1967, rancher George Wheelwright, a wealthy fellow who is credited with co-inventing the Polaroid Land camera, donated to the state a stretch of shoreline at Muir Beach, including the very mouth of Redwood Creek. In 1968, the Brazil Ranch, including a key middle reach of the creek and its tributary Kent Canyon, was added to the state park. But several hundred undeveloped acres just above Muir Beach still remained in private hands.

In 1970, a debate about what to do with some surplus military land around the Golden Gate gave rise to a campaign for a new coastal park to be called the Golden Gate National Recreation Area. The idea started small and finished huge, thanks to public enthusiasm and an expert campaign guided by Wayburn, his conservation colleague Amy Meyer, and San Francisco Congressman Phillip Burton. When President Richard Nixon signed the bill creating the Golden Gate National Recreation Area on October 27, 1972, the new park encompassed 25,000 previously unprotected acres. From the San Francisco waterfront it leaped the Gate and stretched along the Marin County coast to link up with Point Reyes National Seashore, a preserve to the northwest created ten years earlier. The result was an accessible public greenbelt preserving some 108 miles of coastline. It was unmatched in the nation then, and it is unmatched in the nation now.

Along the way, the GGNRA picked up the last private lands in the Redwood Creek watershed, excepting only small developed areas and Green Gulch Farm behind Muir Beach (which rancher Wheelwright had sold to the San Francisco Zen Center). Muir Woods National Monument itself, despite its earlier and separate origin, became part of the GGNRA. With this coup, Wayburn and company had more than fulfilled William Kent's old dream of a national park on Mount Tamalpais.

A look at the map reminds us that the dream was fulfilled in pieces. The very highest point draining to Redwood Creek, the West Peak of Mount Tamalpais, used to be an air force radar station and now belongs to the GGNRA. The rest of the mountain ridgeline is a thin tentacle of Tamalpais State Park. Next down lies a broad swathe of brushy land belonging to the Marin Municipal Water District, though it feeds no reservoir. Next comes Panoramic Highway, and below that the historic core of the state park. Then we have Muir Woods, and then yet more of Tamalpais State Park (the main parking lot and headquarters building at the national monument are actually on land leased from the state). Farther down Redwood Creek, in a final change of ownership, the national recreation area takes over again.

From time to time, there has been talk of consolidating some of the pieces. In the 1960s it was proposed that Muir Woods be swapped to the state as part of a deal creating Redwood National Park on the North Coast. The GGNRA law of 1972 leaned the other way, actually placing Mount Tamalpais State Park inside the new federal park boundaries, just in case the state was tempted to donate the land (and the management costs that go with it). Neither transfer ever occurred.

Like a set of estranged parents with joint custody of a beloved child, the agencies that manage the Redwood Creek watershed have seen the need to work together. In 2003, the National Park Service and the state Department of Parks and Recreation entered into an informal agreement designed, in effect, to erase the boundaries between the parks and treat the region as the single entity it physically is.

Nothing along Redwood Creek speaks so loudly for joint action as the health of the creek itself, with its small and threatened populations of coho salmon and steelhead trout.

The Fate of Redwood Creek

The Miwoks at Muir Beach looked up a valley both similar to and quite different from today's. The basic mosaic of vegetation—coastal scrub on the bluffs, grassland on windy ridges, mixed evergreen forest farther inland, redwoods out of sight in sheltered canyons, bristling chaparral on the steeps of Tamalpais—would have been about the same. But the grasses on the hills back then stayed green all year. Grizzly bears prowled the canyon, and tule elk grazed creekside meadows. Overhead, on their nine-foot wingspans, California condors rode.

Then as now, there was a seasonal lagoon behind the coastal beach, but just upstream of that small estuary a much larger set of dunes impounded a larger body of water, called Big Lagoon on old maps. Brackish in the dry season and fresh in winter and spring, its waters would have been a kind of halfway house where young salmon and trout could feed and adjust their gills and kidneys for the switch from fresh to salt water, a process called smoltification. Big Lagoon was one of the reasons that the historic creek—called Big Lagoon Creek on the oldest maps—had far more fish than today's.

Behind the lagoon, the stream meandered up the flood plain of the lower valley, carving a series of deep pools that would have held water in even the driest autumn. Green Gulch and Kent Canyon may have contributed steadier flows back then. Muir Woods itself would have been a very wild spot then, visited but not dwelt in. (Miwok tradition states there was a seasonal hunting camp at the junction of Fern Creek.) As for the mountaintop above, it was considered a haunted place and would hardly have been set foot upon at all.

Then came the waves of invaders, Spanish, Mexican, Anglo. In 1817, the whole area became part of the domain of the Mission San Rafael. Then or soon after, the Miwoks were removed to the mission, and the land was stocked with European cattle. Though adapted to grazing by elk, the perennial grasses could not withstand the pressure of these larger, omnipresent herds. Native grasses and forbs gave way to annual grasses from the Mediterranean, seeds of which had come with imported animals and their feed. A drought in the 1860s hammered the hills and completed the transition. Since then, the grassy parts of the watershed have mirrored the seasons in the now-classic California manner, turning vivid green when the winter rains come, dying back in the summer to tawny yellow, fading in early autumn to a worn-out, thirsty beige.

Grazing and the change of grasses had another result: a great increase in

soil erosion. The amount of sediment that the stream had to carry increased approximately ninefold. This displaced earth settled first in Big Lagoon. Maps made in 1853 still show this body of water. By 1891, after at least 3,700 years of existence, Big Lagoon was gone. The dunes that had impounded it were later mined out of existence to get sand for use in construction.

A century after the conquest, Redwood Creek nonetheless still supported a major salmon run. Old-timers speak of spawners in Muir Woods "so thick you could barely see the water." There may be an element of exaggeration here, but plainly, the salmon run continued to be counted in hundreds. Today we count in tens.

In the twentieth century, the process of degradation picked up speed. Highways, fire roads, and hillside trails multiplied, each a smaller or larger scratch across the land. The alder and willow trees that had lined the streams were stripped away, depriving the water of shade and the fish of shelter and of insect food. At the same time, stream flows grew "flashier": less water flowed in the creek in summer, but more came gushing down in winter storms. Redwood Creek responded by cutting deeper into the soil, burying itself in a trench, cut off from the flood plain it had regularly inundated in the past; this led to a further acceleration of flows and yet more erosion. The logging of the redwoods in Kent Canyon, around 1960, certainly added to the burden on Redwood Creek. Near the mouth of the stream, the process took another form as eroded sediments settled out, causing the streambed to fill up or "aggrade" and increasing local flooding.

Even the parks in the upper part of the watershed contributed to flooding and erosion. Since 1928, Panoramic Highway has been a major source of sediment. In Muir Woods itself, foot traffic killed off streamside vegetation, misguided maintenance robbed the creek of the logs that trapped spawning gravels and formed pools, and well-meant engineering armored banks, hurrying floodwaters on downstream.

With all this mauling, the surprising thing isn't that coho salmon and steelhead trout in Redwood Creek diminished. It's astonishing that they continued to make it up to spawn at Muir Woods at all.

The Other Redwoods

When Muir Woods National Monument was created, it was one of three pockets of old-growth redwoods on the ocean flank of Mount Tamalpais. The two others have had contrasting fates.

Just over the ridge toward Stinson Beach is a precipitous valley aptly named Steep Ravine. Its upper reaches contain an unlogged redwood forest smaller than Muir Woods but charmingly situated along a dashing stream. This area, too, belonged to the Kent family; William Kent once planned to use it for an extension of the Mountain Railroad to Stinson Beach. When that idea faded, he sought to give the land to Muir Woods National Monument. His gift was not accepted, however, for an interesting reason: he reserved the right to dam the creek for the benefit of the town below. The park service did not want land so encumbered, though it gratefully accepted his gift of some other acreage nearby.

How could Kent, who had given Muir Woods to the nation to block one dam, hold out for the right to build another, now calling scenery "a lower use"? William Kent described himself as a conservationist, not a preservationist. He was always looking to balance needs and resources. In his mind, the balance at Steep Ravine was different: the forest at stake less spectacular, the need for water from the site greater. As in the intense debate about the Hetch Hetchy dam in Yosemite National Park, he felt that—this time—public water supply was the greater of two competing goods.

View from Mt. Tamalpais, 1934

In any case, the dam in upper Steep Ravine was never built, and Kent wound up donating the land, not to the federal government, but to the new Mount Tamalpais State Park.

History was unkinder to the redwood forest in a valley that now bears William Kent's name: Kent Canyon, a tributary of Redwood Creek that feeds the parent stream below the monument, halfway to the sea. Kent actually owned this property for a time. He bought what was then called Rocky Canyon in about 1910 as an additional buffer for Muir Woods. But after his death it was sold off again.

Around 1960, it was thoroughly logged. Almost nothing is known about this lost redwood stand. Was it still virgin forest at mid-century? Might it have been almost a peer to Muir Woods, a Hetch Hetchy to the Yosemite Valley of the national monument? It is a haunting thought that so large and accessible a forest fell to the tractor and the saw a few years before the green tide of expanding parkland reached the site.

Rachel Carson Visits

Carson, circa 1940

Rachel Carson, the biologist and author whose book *Silent Spring* alerted the world to the hazards of pesticides and is credited with triggering the modern environmental movement, always wanted to visit Muir Woods. In the spring of 1964, two years after the publication of *Silent Spring* and weeks before her death of cancer, she made it, in a wheelchair, in the company of Sierra Club Executive Director David Brower and his wife, Anne. To a friend Carson wrote:

"Once over the Golden Gate Bridge one climbs up and up into those smooth brown hills, so much of the road lined with eucalyptus trees . . . Then a long winding descent, one hairpin curve after another, into the canyon where the redwoods are . . . one sees great, burned-out stumps here and there, looking fresh enough to have resulted from a fire last year; yet the ranger said there had been no fire in Muir Woods for at least 150 years . . . There was a marvelous freshness in the air, though I couldn't detect a distinctive odor. The under story of these woods is chiefly the California laurel—a huge tree . . . Perfectly huge oxalis is a predominant ground cover and there are marvelous ferns, sword especially."

Besides the redwoods, Carson visited the beach at Rodeo Cove just outside the Golden Gate, now also part of the Golden Gate National Recreation Area. She studied the many-colored crystals in the sand and admired, with foreboding, a magnificent flight of California brown pelicans. The pesticide DDT caused pelicans to lay thin-shelled eggs that broke when the parents brooded; populations had already crashed in the eastern U.S.; the turn of the West was coming. In the 1970 season, just one California pelican would successfully fledge. But the sometimes painful learning process begun with *Silent Spring* was all the while progressing, and in 1972 DDT was banned in the U.S. Thanks in no small measure to Rachel Carson, we can still see on these coasts the flocks that she saw on that poignant spring day.

Those who contemplate the beauty of the earth find reserves of strength that will endure as long as life lasts.

Rachel Carson

The Dipsea Race

Every June, Muir Woods National Monument is host to a tradition four years older than the monument itself: the Dipsea Race from Mill Valley to Stinson Beach, second-oldest footrace in America after the Boston Marathon.

The Dipsea was first run in 1904, informally and on the spur of the moment, as a friendly rivalry between members of San Francisco's Olympic Club. Since 1905 it has been an organized tradition, suspended only in the depths of the Depression and during World War II and run unofficially even then.

The course covers 7.1 miles and goes up (and down) 2,000 feet of hills. Shortly after the Mill Valley start, runners pump up a staircase of 676 steps. From the crest above Muir Woods, a plunging stretch known as "Suicide" brings them down to the monument entrance. They clatter across the Redwood Creek bridge and ascend to the Deer Park ridgetop, bordering the park on the south side. "Half Way Rock" here is the traditional midpoint of the race in elapsed time. The route continues with the further ascent called "Cardiac Hill" (of course), "The

Swoop" down into the narrow canyon of Steep Ravine (with mossy rocks and ladders), a final slight rise called "Insult Hill," and the Stinson Beach finish line. In the first few years, the runners went a bit farther on the sand to reach the Dipsea Tavern, the race's long-gone namesake. The course record is some 42 minutes; the first hundred or so people make it in less than one hour. Older and pre-adult runners get head starts based on their age.

In 1920, Ellen Reiman won a companion event, the Women's Dipsea Hike. Held from 1918 to 1922, the hike attracted more competitors than the men's race.

Women were always interested in running the Dipsea. In 1918, a women's race was instituted, but soon halted because churches objected to skimpy costumes. Astonishingly, the race did not go coed until 1971—and had its first female winner in 1973, a ten-year-old girl.

Originally, the Dipsea had no fixed course; runners could choose their own way through the web of trails on the flanks of Mount Tamalpais, and even make shortcuts between them. But over the years, the most efficient route emerged, and park managers have lately frowned on innovation. With such large numbers—the race once topped 2,000 participants and is now capped at 1,500—erosion and disturbance of wildlife have to be taken into account. The Dipsea Trail gets extra maintenance to handle the crowds.

Restoring Redwood Creek

The year 1960 was the approximate low point for the health of this watershed. With the spread of parks and the gradual cessation of grazing, the trend has since been upward. Average erosion rates have subsided from about nine times to about five times the natural background level. Channel dredging, which continued into the 1980s, has ceased. Willows and alders are once again shading and cooling streams. In Mount Tamalpais State Park and in Muir Woods, the creek is gradually reworking its banks toward a more natural state. But the continuing low numbers of salmon, compared with more primitive streams, make it clear how much improvement is still possible.

The solution is to restore the creek to a more naturally functioning channel and floodplain system.

In 2003, the landowners along Redwood Creek sat down together to identify what was still limiting the stream and what more could be done to fix it.

High on the list were erosion-prone stretches of trail and fire road that could be upgraded, moved, or simply abandoned. You can see one result a mile below the Muir Woods entrance, where Franks Valley Road crosses Redwood Creek. A track that once reached the waterline is now gated off, greening up, and cordoned by an arc of ropy erosion control material. Repeat this scene a few dozen times, and you can see the healing of a lacerated land.

The 2003 study found much damage coming from old culverts, the pipes where major and minor roads cross major and minor streams. Many of these had been built small and tended to back up, overflow, and even rip out in winter rains; some also blocked the passage of fish. The largest of many culvert replacement projects came in 2007, when the big tube that conveyed Kent Canyon Creek under Franks Valley Road into Redwood Creek was torn out and replaced with a larger open-bottomed passageway. This provides both a more generous and a more natural path for an important spawning stream.

The stretch of Redwood Creek downstream from this junction is particularly troublesome. This is the reach that came into public ownership latest and also the segment most profoundly modified over the years: dredged, straightened, leveed, and—near Muir Beach—completely shifted out of its natural course and confined by a levee to make room for valley-bottom agriculture. Two inadequate road dikes and the Muir Beach parking lot (expanded and raised in the 1980s by the National Park Service itself) further constrain the stream.

Today the creek is quite obviously getting ready to break these shackles. It is working to carve new meanders, develop new flood plains, overtop levees. The challenge is not to stop these changes but to manage them. At one site, it sufficed to remove a superfluous levee, allowing the stream to loop out into a former commercial flower field. At another site nearby, heavy equipment was brought in to reshape one bank of a deeply incised stream segment, giving it room to evolve.

The biggest project will be at the very mouth of the stream. Stuffed with sediment and hemmed in by a levee, this stretch regularly rebels and inundates the roads and structures that people have placed around it. The solution is to restore the creek to a more naturally functioning channel and floodplain system. Bridges and parking lot will also be modified to leave room for natural flows. Thus freed, the creek should be able to scour out its bed where it needs to and carry sediment out to sea.

Thought has been given to a more dramatic solution: restoring the old Big Lagoon. This vision proves impractical, however. There are simply too many things in the way. Moreover, as long as the watershed continues to erode at several times the natural rate, the new wetland would be a temporary feature, doomed to fill in over time. The old balance cannot be recreated. But a new one can perhaps be achieved.

View of the lower Redwood Creek watershed from Dias Ridge Trail

Muir Woods in the World

From a fish's-eye view, Redwood Creek is the vital corridor into and out of Muir Woods. A spotted owl would see things differently. For the owl, what matters is the presence of other suitable forests nearby in which mates can be found and into which young can disperse.

Biologists studying oceanic islands have long noted a match between size and biotic wealth: the larger the area of an island, the higher the count of species it supports. Even on the mainland, today's parks and preserves are islands of a sort, cut off by expanses not of water but of land that particular species can no longer use. Muir Woods alone, if surrounded by development, would be far too small an island to sustain itself. The Golden Gate National Recreation Area and the associated public lands make up an island of much more respectable size, but even this is vulnerable: to waves of exotic species and diseases, to the genetic decay that afflicts isolated populations of animals, and, of course, to global effects like accelerated climate change.

Along Redwood Creek, scientists and managers are alert to two possible results of climate change. One is sea level rise. If this is rapid, it could upset calculations for the mouth of Redwood Creek—though the stream itself would adjust more readily than people dependent on low-lying houses and roads.

The second possible effect, far more profound for Muir Woods and for the redwoods in general, would be any change in the timing and moisture content of summer fog. We owe the mist to a zone of cold water just offshore, itself the product of a pattern of winds and currents that might alter. Will a generally warming sea mean more fog, less fog, or not much change at all? Computer models, not very good at predicting what will happen in a particular small locale, give no clear answer. Any large decrease in fog would be very bad news for the ancient trees, especially here in the southern and drier part of their territory. Though they have shifted their ground before and could again—even now they are gradually extending into Oregon—the redwoods might suffer a net shrinkage of range.

The World in Muir Woods

The coast redwoods impress human beings so much that we seek meanings there for ourselves. William Kent got a whole morality out of them. "'Stand straight and strong who can,' say the redwoods, 'protect and shelter the weak.' . . . Long life, well lived, strength and resultant quietness; modesty, courage, beauty and the kindliness of infinite hospitality!" Religious overtones are often present. There is bound to be a Cathedral Grove.

In June of 1944, with the end of World War II in sight, President Franklin D. Roosevelt met with the one surviving savior of Muir Woods, the eighty-year-old Gifford Pinchot. Pinchot wanted a world conference on conservation, to be held at the national monument "as a basis of permanent peace." The following February, Interior Secretary Harold Ickes proposed a variant of the idea: the diplomats who had convened in San Francisco to launch the United Nations should hold a session in Muir Woods. "The delegates could gain a perspective and sense of time that could be obtained nowhere in America better than in such a forest... Muir Woods is a cathedral, the pillars of which have stood through much of recorded human history."

Then President Roosevelt died, and the meeting occurred as a memorial in his honor, attended by the delegates—and held, of course, at Cathedral Grove (see photo, right).

World peace is as elusive as ever, but Muir Woods remains a good place to think as well as to learn and feel. And the object of such a meditation, today and in this place, almost has to be the natural world, our dominating place in it, our pervasive effect upon it, and our resulting sense of responsibility for it.

Looking back at one hundred years of Muir Woods National Monument, and at two hundred years of accelerated human impact on its surroundings, shall we feel pride or shame? Active we have certainly been, improving, degrading, exploiting, modifying, misunderstanding, appreciating, and also saving. We have proved, if it needed proving, our tendency to undervalue and throw away what Nature has given us. We have also demonstrated what does indeed need proving: that we have in us the ability to learn other, gentler, and more thoughtful ways.

Muir Woods National Monument, the Redwood Creek basin, even the Golden Gate National Recreation Area: all might be described as testing grounds for much greater efforts that must come. In the next decades on our planet, both environmental destruction and attempts at restoration are bound

to reach new levels. No one can say how satisfactory the balance of those forces will be. Certainly our learning powers will be called upon as never before.

Muir Woods is a place to acknowledge, somberly, that the odds of achieving decent human life in an ecologically healthy world are not all that good. It is also a place to acknowledge, humbly and thankfully, just how much better we can do, when we try.

And another idea comes poking slyly in. As Ickes pointed out, Muir Woods is a place to take the very long view. If it teaches the fragility of nature, this forest equally teaches its resilience. These salmon have survived a century of stream mismanagement. These redwoods have survived not only our well-meaning, sometimes blundering efforts, but a hundred million years of climate change, geological upheaval, even (it is believed) the catastrophic meteorite impact that ended the reign of the dinosaurs.

In the shadow of these great trees, we can allow ourselves this oddly comforting suspicion: maybe we are not quite so important as we thought.

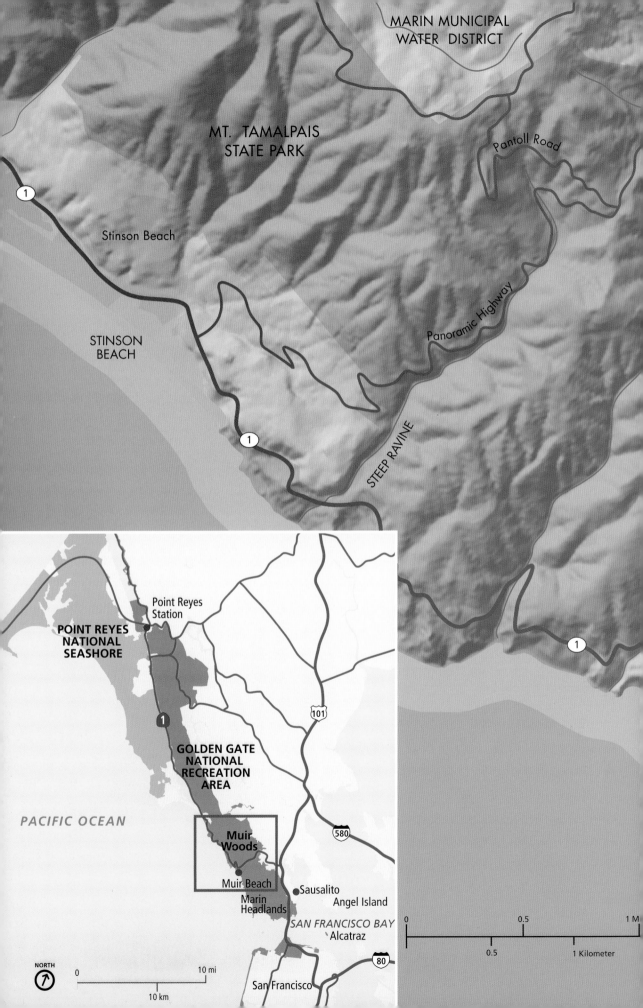

MARIN MUNICIPAL
WATER DISTRICT

MT. TAMALPAIS
STATE PARK

Pantoll Road

1

Stinson Beach

STINSON
BEACH

Panoramic Highway

STEEP RAVINE

1

1

POINT REYES
NATIONAL
SEASHORE

Point Reyes
Station

101

GOLDEN GATE
NATIONAL
RECREATION
AREA

PACIFIC OCEAN

Muir
Woods

580

Muir Beach

Marin
Headlands

Sausalito

Angel Island

SAN FRANCISCO BAY

Alcatraz

80

San Francisco

NORTH

0   10 mi

0   10 km

0   0.5   1 M

0.5   1 Kilometer

Suggested Reading

To delve more deeply into the topics of Muir Woods National Monument, coast redwoods, John Muir, and local Mill Valley history, see the following.

Muir Woods National Monument

Joseph, Stephen. *Muir Woods Meditations* (San Francisco: Golden Gate National Parks Conservancy, 2009). A small book with a large visual impact; Joseph's photographs are accompanied by a variety of inspiring quotes.

Khosla, Maya. *Web of Water: Life in Redwood Creek* (San Francisco: Golden Gate National Parks Conservancy, 1997). Scientifically grounded and lyrically written examination of Muir Woods' Redwood Creek.

Morley, James M. *Muir Woods: The Ancient Redwood Forest Near San Francisco* (San Francisco: Smith-Morley, 1991). A well-researched and highly illustrated book with more than 70 photos, diagrams, and maps.

Coast Redwoods

Barbour, Michael, Marjorie Popper, John Evarts, eds. *Coast Redwoods, A Natural and Cultural History* (Los Olivos, CA: Cachuma Press, 2001). Deeply informative and richly illustrated story of the biology, ecology, and cultural history of *Sequoia sempervirens*.

Dewitt, John B. *California Redwood Parks and Preserves: A Guide to the Redwood Parks and a Brief History of the Efforts to Save the Redwoods* (San Francisco: Save-the-Redwoods League, 1993). This 38-page booklet is an excellent introduction to Save-the-Redwoods League and the redwood state parks.

Eifert, Larry. *Eifert's Nature Guide: California's Coast Redwoods* (Port Townsend, WA: Estuary Press, 2006). This guide packs a lot of information into its 32 pages, covering the birds, animals, and plants most commonly found in California's coast redwood forests.

Lyons, Kathleen and Mary Beth Cuneo-Lazaneo. *Plants of the Coast Redwood Region* (Los Altos, CA: Looking Press, 1988). Field guide to plants commonly found in the coast redwood forests; color photographs and non-technical text describe many of the region's trees, shrubs, herbaceous plants, and ferns.

Noss, Reed F., ed. *The Redwood Forest: History, Ecology, and Conservation of the Coast Redwoods* (Washington DC: Island Press, 2000). Offers a case study for ecosystem-level conservation and explains how redwood forests function.

Preston, Richard. *Wild Trees: A Story of Passion and Daring* (New York: Random House, 2008). There's an entire primeval world in the treetops of a redwood forest. In addition to its adventure-story aspects, the book discusses the history of old-growth forests and explains forest-floor and canopy ecology.

John Muir
Ehrlich, Gretel. *John Muir, Nature's Visionary* (Washington, DC: National Geographic Books, 2000). Now out of print, this richly illustrated book is worth looking for. Ehrlich focuses on Muir's "unquenchable" appetite for life and learning and quotes widely from his works, including unpublished journals.

Stetson, Lee, ed. *The Wild Muir: 22 of John Muir's Greatest Adventures* (Berkeley, CA: Heyday Books, 1994). Showcases both Muir's writing talents and his taste for hair-raising adventures.

Teale, Edwin Way, ed. *The Wilderness World of John Muir* (Boston: Houghton Mifflin Company, 2001). This collection captures what it was like to wander without gun or sleeping bag through a wild and unsettled America.

White, Fred D., ed. *Essential John Muir: A Selection of John Muir's Best Writings* (Berkeley, CA: Heyday Books, 2006). Includes some of the best of John Muir's writings on nature as well as his thoughts on religion and society.

Wolfe, Linnie Marsh. *Son of the Wilderness: The Life of John Muir* (Madison, WI: University of Wisconsin Press, 2003). This book was originally published in 1945 and is based in large part on the author's personal interviews with people who knew and worked with Muir.

Worster, Donald. *A Passion for Nature: The Life of John Muir* (New York: Oxford University Press, 2008). A comprehensive biography covering the full scope and sweep of the life of America's greatest conservationist.

Local History
Chalmers, Claudine. *Images of America: Early Mill Valley* (Charleston, SC: Arcadia Publishing, 2005). A well-chosen collection of photos and a short history of Mill Valley from the days of the native people through World War II.

Spitz, Barry. *Mill Valley: The Early Years* (San Anselmo, CA: Potrero Meadow Publishing, 1996). Includes maps, vintage black-and-white photos, and the in-depth story of Mill Valley's evolution and development through the 1930s. Read it to find out more about William Kent's purchase of Redwood Canyon (later named Muir Woods) and the Mount Tamalpais Railway, the "crookedest railroad in the world."

Photography Credits

Many of the photographs included in this book are protected by copyright and/or require permission to reproduce. For more information, please contact the source.

Frontis: Robert Campbell (fog over Mt. Tamalpais)

p. 16: Miguel.v/Wikimedia Commons (right/General Grant tree)

p. 19: National Portrait Gallery, Smithsonian Institution

p. 26: Brenda Tharp

p. 48: Mike Baird/Flickr.bairdphotos.com (top/darner); © 2008 Gary McDonald (bottom/buckeye)

p. 49: © 2008 Gary McDonald (top right/echo blue); randomtruth/Flickr (middle left/pale swallowtail); T.W. Davies © California Academy of Sciences (bottom/anglewing)

p. 50: CSU Chico/Big Chico Creek Ecological Reserve (top/Ensatina samalander)

p. 51: Mason Cummings

p. 52: randomtruth/Flickr (middle left/woodrat); John Good (middle right/deer mouse); Franco Folini/Wikimedia Commons (top left/gray squirrel)

p. 53: Gillian Bowser/Wikimedia Commons (bottom right/pocket gopher); Wildlife Associates (bottom left/mountain lion)

p. 60: Bryant Olsen (left/hoary bat)

p. 61: John & Karen Hollingsworth/USFWS (right/northern spotted owl)

p. 62: Dawn Vornholt

p. 63: Ron Wolf (top/olive-sided flycatcher); Andrew Brownsword/Wikimedia Commons (bottom/pileated woodpecker)

p. 64: Lee Karney/USFWS (top left/Steller's jay); Stephen Dowlan (bottom left/raven); NPS (right/snowy egret)

p. 65: Stephen Dowlan (top left/winter wren); C. Schlawe/USFWS (top right/belted kingfisher); Larry Selman/www.MostlyBirds.com (bottom left/Swainson's thrush); Donna Dewhurst/USFWS (bottom middle/Wilson's warbler)

p. 66: Ron Wolf (top right/varied thrush)

p. 67: Lee Karney/USFWS (bottom right/scrub jay); Bill Raymond/www.projectnation.net (top/heron)

p. 68: Larry Selman/www.MostlyBirds.com (middle right/Pacific slope flycatcher); Donna Dewhurst/USFWS (bottom left/ruby-crowned kinglet); Ron Wolf (bottom right/Oregon junco)

p. 71: Cacophony/Wikimedia Commons (right/coho smolt); Jerome Charaoui/Wikimedia Commons (left/jumping salmon)

p. 73: Eric Engbretson/USFWS (right/steelhead trout)

pp. 74–75: Robert Campbell

p. 79: National Park Service Historic Photograph Collection

pp. 80–81: Annals of the Bohemian Club

p. 93: Francis M. Fritz/Wikimedia Commons

p. 99: Courtesy Mill Valley Historical Society (left/Laura White); Courtesy Ann Arnold (right/Elizabeth Kent)

p. 100: California Academy of Sciences (Alice Eastwood); M. Simmonson/USFS (top/manzanita)

p. 118: Randy Smith/Wikimedia Commons

p. 119: © Neal Kramer (bottom/wild ginger, yerba buena)

p. 128: Mason Cummings

p. 138: USFWS

p. 144–145: Mason Cummings

p. 149: Save-the-Redwoods League

p. 158: David Sanger (John Hart); John Calaway (Edgar Wayburn)

Al Greening: pp. 8; 10–12; 14–15; 27; 28; 29 (top left/honey mushroom, middle/trees); 37 (top/Redwood Creek); 44; 46; 49 (top left/painted lady butterfly, middle right/pipevine swallowtail butterfly); 52 (bottom/chipmunk); 54–55; 57; 66 (bottom/ravens); 72–73 (top/Fern Creek), 98–99; 101; 123

Stephen Joseph: pp. v; viii; x–xi; 2-6; 9; 16 (left); 18; 29 (bottom/golden waxy cap); 30; 32–35; 37 (bottom/Redwood Creek); 38–39; 42; 50 (bottom/banana slug); 56; 116; 119 (top/lady fern); 120; 124; 126–127; 132–133; 139; 143; 147; 150–151

Matt Knoth: pp. 52 (top right/bobcat); 53 (top/coyote); 65 (bottom right/goldfinch); 66 (middle/red-tailed hawk, top left/hermit thrush); 67 (bottom left/spotted towhee, middle/great horned owlet); 68 (top/white-crowned sparrow); 69

Alice Kong: pp. 20 (trees); 24–25; 29 (top right/oyster mushroom); 45; 47; 59; 60 (right/tree trunk); 70; 76–77; 135

Park Archives and Record Center/Golden Gate National Recreation Area: pp. vi–vii; xii; 22 (Len Chapman/foggy morning); 40 (CCC Fern Creek, 1934); 41 (CCC clearing brush); 43; 72 (left/salmon); 78; 82; 84; 85 (top/original Muir Woods Inn); 86–91; 94–97; 102–103; 104 (bottom/gravity ride); 105; 106–108; 110–115; 131; 136–137 (L. Moe/panorama from Mt. Tamalpais); 140–141 (Dipsea runners)

John Hart is the author of a dozen books as well as a poet and mountain climber. Among his accolades are the James D. Phelan Award, the Commonwealth Club Medal (twice), and the David R. Brower Award for Service in the Field of Conservation. In his non-fiction work, he focuses primarily on water policy, farmland conservation, land-use planning, and backpacking and climbing. He lives in northern California.
www.johnhart.com

Edgar Wayburn (1906–2010) played a major role in protecting literally millions of acres of American wilderness concurrently with practicing medicine, which he did for more than fifty years. Considered by many to be a modern-day John Muir, Dr. Wayburn received the Presidential Medal of Freedom from President Bill Clinton in 1999.
www.sierraclub.org/history/wayburn/